Deaths

from the

FEDERAL UNION

1830-1850

෧ඐ෧

(Baldwin County, Georgia)

By: Rev. Silas Emmett Lucas, Jr.

Please direct all correspondence and orders to:

www.southernhistoricalpress.com
or
SOUTHERN HISTORICAL PRESS, Inc.
PO BOX 1267
375 West Broad Street
Greenville, SC   29601
southernhistoricalpress@gmail.com

ISBN #0-89308-603-7

Printed in the United States of America

31 July 1830

Died in Monroe county, on the 8th instant, MRS. ELIZA SMITH, consort of George Smith of Macon, and daughter of John Evans of Monroe county, aged 19 years.

Died at the house of Gen. David Blackshear, on the evening of the 2d July, COL. JOSEPH BLACKSHEAR, of Laurens county, Geo. in the 55th year of his age.

A man by the name of AUSTIN, a negro speculator, lately from Virginia, was killed near Clinton some short time ago, by the kick of a horse... (Macon Telegraph, July 24)

7 August 1830

Died at the Indian Spring on the 30th of July last, WILLIAM MOUGHON, of Jones county, in the 27th year of his age. He left a wife and one child.

14 August 1830

Died in Milledgeville on the morning of the 5th inst., COL. ROBERT R. RUFFIN, aged 42 years. His disease, the dropsy of the heart and lungs, was lingering. Was an officer in the Army during the late war with Great Britain. After having been some time in the service, he was made Aid to Gen. Gaines, and was engaged in several battles. Has left a bereaved widow and two fine boys. (with short eulogy)

21 August 1830

Died on the 9th instant, near Greensboro, MRS. ELIZABETH RANDALL, daughter of Mr. Vincent Sanford, aged 20 years.

4 September 1830

Died in this place on Wednesday last, THOMAS DOVER, son of PRYOR and MARGARET WRIGHT, aged 4 years 9 months and 15 days. (short eulogy)

Information wanted. If any person in Alabama, or elsewhere, knows any thing of the death of a man whose name was THOMAS SANDERSON HUFTY, who is believed to have deceased some where in Alabama, between two and three years ago, and will communicate the same to Rev. Dr. E.S. Ely of Philadelphia, they will much oblige a relative of the deceased, and serve the cause of humanity. (Signed Martha Calver).

It may be proper to call the attention of our readers to the fate of WM. HOLLINGSWORTH who perished in a well near the State-House in this town, on Wednesday last. He fell a sacrifice in attempting to descend into a well containing carbonic acid gas...

11 September 1830

Died on Saturday the 28th ult., at her residence near Lawrenceville, Gwinnett county, MRS. RACHEL KENNEY, after a short illness, aged 53 years, formerly of Edgefield district, S.C. and for many years a member of the Methodist Church.

25 September 1830

    Died at the residence of her father, near Manchester on the 14th inst.
MRS. MARY REBECCA McDUFFIE, consort of the Hon. George McDuffie, and
daughter of Richard Singleton, Esq.

2 October 1830

    Died near Milledgeville on the morning of the 20th Sept.
MRS. SARAH A. CHENEY, of South Carolina.

    Died in Macon on the 24th ult. ALBERT G. CLOPTON, Esq. a native of
Henrico co. Virginia, aged about 32 years. (short eulogy).
(Macon Messenger)

    Died at his residence in Hancock county on the 1st inst. the
REV. EDMUND SHACKLEFORD, aged 49 years, two months and 29 days.
(long eulogy) (Southern Recorder)

    Died at Auburn on the 12th inst. the Right Rev. JOHN HENRY HOBART, D.D.,
Bishop of the Diocese of New York. (short eulogy)

16 October 1830

    Another soldier of the Revolution gone! Died at his residence near
Forsyth, Monroe county, on the 6th inst. JOHN WATSON, senr. Esq. in
his 86th year. He was a native of Scotland, but when a boy of twelve,
left his parents and friends in the year 57, and came to this country.
He served through the war of the Revolution as a private soldier, and proved
himself a true Whig.

6 November 1830

    Died in Monticello, Jasper county, on Saturday the 23d ult. REV. JAMES E.
HINES, of Burk county, aged 42; an orderly and devoted Christian since
about his 13th year; attached to the Baptist Denomination. (short eulogy).

13 November 1830

    Departed this life on the 8th inst., in the 15th month of his age,
THOMAS F. GREEN, only child of Thomas F. and Adeline E. A. Green of this place.

27 November 1830

    It gives us great pain to announce the death of General DAVID R. WILLIAMS,
of S.C. His death was occasioned by the fall of a piece of timber, which
broke both legs, and occasioned his death the next day.

11 December 1830

    (From the National Gazette). Died on the 22nd instant, at the residence of
Col. Armstrong, in Nashville, of a pulmonary complaint, JEFFREY LOCKELIER, a
free man of color commonly called Major Jeffrey, aged about 42 years. The
deceased resided in that town for upwards of twenty years. He was present
at almost every battle that was fought during the last war. He was in the
Creek country during the whole of that war, and participated in the battles
of Enotechopo, Emuckfa, and the Horse Shoe, and he was distinguished for his
valor in the bloody conflict between the artillery and the Indians at the
former place. He followed the standard of General Jackson to the siege of
Orleans, and participated in the action of the 23d as well as that of the
glorious 8th. At the breaking out of the Seminole war he again took the
field, and was at Sewanny, the surrender of Fort St. Mark, and the assaults
on Pensacola and the Barrancas. His military service terminated only when
his country ceased to have enemies.

18 December 1830

    (From the Augusta Chronicle). MRS. MARY McTYRE departed this life
at Smith Vale, the residence of her brother, A. Rhodes, Esq.,
in Richmond co. on the 20th ult. in the 69th year of her age; having
been a regular and pious member of the Methodist Episcopal Church
upwards of 40 years. (short eulogy)

25 December 1830

    Died in Hillsborough, N.C. on the 12th ultimo, JOHN UMSTEAD TAYLOR,
eldest son of Major John Taylor. Was in the 21st year of his age, a
student of the university of this state, and attached to the junior
class. (long eulogy) (Recorder)

1 January 1831

    Died suddenly in Milledgeville on the 26th December, MR. CHARLES C.
BIRCH, of apoplexy. He was in fine health the day before he was taken,
and survived the shock but three days. Has left a distressed widow
and children.

8 January 1831

    Died in this county on Wednesday morning, 5th instant, in the 70th year
of his age, WILLIAM P. BROWN, Esq. a Revolutionary soldier.

    Died in the county of Bibb, on Sunday the 19th ultimo, MRS. SARAH
CROWDER, wife of Mr. John Crowder, in the 32d year of her age.

15 January 1831

    Died at his residence near Carnesville, Ga. on the 21st December,
JOHN STUBBS, Sen. in the 54th year of his age.

1 February 1831

    Died at the residence of Dr. James Thweatt of Monroe county, on the
21st inst., MR. JAMES THWEATT, eldest son of the Reverend Thomas Thweatt
of Clinton. He embraced religion at a Camp Meeting about eighteen
months since, and became a member of the Methodist Episcopal Church.
(Christian Repertory)

    PETER FRANCISCO, a distinguished revolutionary soldier, died lately
in Virginia, about 70 years of age. He was sergeant at arms to the
House of Delegates of that State - and the Legislature paid deserved
honor to his memory.

8 February 1831

    Died on the 31st ult. MRS. LOUISA WOOLFOLK, aged 30 years, relict of
Mr. Austin Woolfolk, late of this city. (short eulogy)
(Augusta Chronicle)

    Died at her father's residence in the county of Columbia on the 22d inst.
MRS. JUDGE REID, the only daughter of Robert Randolph, Esq. aged thirty
seven years and two months. (short eulogy)

15 February 1831
 Memorial resolution on the death of PETER FRANCISCO taken from the
 Richmond Enquirer.

22 February 1831
 Died at Zebulon, Pike county, on the 13th inst. MRS. MARTHA W. BLACKBURN,
 aged 27 years, wife of Dr. John L. Blackburn.

 Died in Macon on the 13th inst. MR. THOMAS P. CARNES, aged 21 years and
 eleven months, son of Judge Carnes, late of Athens.

8 March 1831
 Died on the 12th February, NATHAN BRADY, JUN. of Stewart county, formerly
 a Representative of Randolph County in the Georgia Legislature. Mr. Brady
 left home on the 10th for Troup County, and after riding about 20 miles
 up the river towards Columbus, he stopped to let his horse drink at a
 creek called Hitcheta, and while there he received a rifle ball of a large
 size, which centered back of the left shoulder, passed under the collar
 bone, cutting the wind pipe, and came out the right side of his neck. On
 receiving the ball he fell forward, but the horse raising his head at the
 moment, caught him on his neck and prevented his falling off. He held on
 to his horse and rode about 3 miles to the nearest house, where he lingered
 until about 1 o'clock on the 12th, when he expired. It is supposed that
 he was shot by an Indian, but this fact is not yet proven. (Telegraph).

15 March 1831
 Death notice of WYATT FOARD, Esq. Was sudden and unexpected. On Monday,
 the 7th instant, he was seized by sensations which assured him that death
 was upon him - summoned his wife and children around - bade them an
 everlasting adieu - and in an hour, was in eternity. (short eulogy)

24 March 1831
 Died on Sunday the 27th of February, in Morgan county, MRS. TILOTHY WALTON,
 wife of Peter W. Walton, aged 24 years. For several years previous to her
 death, she was a member of the Baptist Church. (short eulogy)

 Departed this life on Friday the 11th instant, after a violent attack of
 an inflammatory fever, which he bore for a little more than eight days,
 CAPT. GOODWIN MYRICK of Baldwin county, in the 52d year of his age. He had
 been an exemplary member of the Methodist Church for nearly 20 years; left
 bereaved wife and children.

21 April 1831
 Died in this place on Monday 4th April, of consumption, MR. THOMAS C. CLAY,
 of Bourbon county, Ky., aged about 26 years.

 Died on the 18th instant after a short illness, VIRGINIA, the youngest
 daughter of A.B. and JANE FANNIN of Savannah, aged 19 months and five days.

28 April 1831
 Died on the 15th instant at his residence in Jones county, JAMES A DELAUNAY, Sen.
 in the 70th year of his age. He was a native of France, but emigrated to this
 country in early life.

 Died in Clinton, Jones county, on the 17th inst. URIAH PETERSON, youngest
 son of the Rev. THOMAS THWEATT, aged 15 months.

4

12 May 1831
  Died in this place on Wednesday night the 4th instant, SARAH ELIZABETH,
  youngest daughter of MR. ROBERT McCOMB, aged 1 year 2 months 9 days.

  Died in Hancock county on the 25th ult. in the 21st year of her age,
  MRS. JULIA ANN FOARD, consort of Maj. William P. Foard.

  Died on the 4th of April, of a most intractable, acute disease,
  at his residence in Houston county, MR. STERLING LISON, late of Twiggs
  county, aged 32 years. He was a native of North Carolina and emigrated
  to this State in 1821. He was left an orphan at an early age, and
  commenced the world very poor... (short eulogy)
  (The papers at Raleigh, N.C. and the Floridian will please reprint).

9 June 1831
  Died in this place on Sunday evening 5th inst., after an illness of
  eighteen days, WILLIAM COOK, aged 7 years and 3 months, youngest son of
  Maj. Philip Cook.

  Died on the 22d of May, MATHEW MARSHALL of Jones county.

23 June 1831
  Died on the 16th instant near Waynesborough, in Burke county,
  MRS. MARIA M. MORRIS, relict of the late James E. Morris, Esq., in the
  52d year of her age. Was a native of South Carolina; member of the
  Presbyterian Church. (with eulogy)

30 June 1831
  Died at Augusta on the 9th instant, MR. THOMAS QUIZENBERRY, Sen. a native
  of Virginia, but for the last 26 years a resident of Augusta, aged 54 years.

  Died in Augusta on the 26th instant, in the 39th year of her age,
  MRS. MARTHA DILLON, wife of William C. Dillon, Esq. of that city.

7 July 1831
  Died in Zebulon, Pike county, on Monday the 27th of June, MRS. MARY ANN NEAL,
  aged 19 years, wife of John Neal, merchant, of Zebulon.

14 July 1831
  Another revolutionary patriot gone! Died at his residence a few days since,
  in Henry county, MR. JOHN WYATT, aged 93 years... (with eulogy)

11 August 1831
  Died in this place on the night of the 5th instant, MR. PATRICK O'BRIEN,
  a native of Ireland, aged about 27 years.

  Died in Coweta county, Ga. on the 31st ultimo, FLORA ANN SPEAN, only
  daughter of Major William A. Spean, aged 2 years 4 months.

18 August 1831
  Died in this place on Saturday night last, ABRAHAM FANNIN, youngest child
  of DR. TOMLINSON FORT, aged 19 months.

  Died in Twiggs county on the 28th ultimo, at night, of a protracting and
  unrelenting cephalitis, in the 26th year of her age, MRS. NANCY DUPREE,
  consort of Dr. Ira E. Dupree. (with eulogy)

SAMUEL WILLIAMS, a Revolutionary soldier, died at his residence in Bulloch county on the 4th of July last. He completed the seventy-second year of his age on the day before his death. For several years previous to his death, he was a member of the Baptist Church. (short eulogy)

1 September 1831

Departed this life on 26th July, at his residence in Baldwin County, JESSE DOLES, Sen. in his 80th year; a Soldier of the Revolution, and for between forty-five and fifty years, had been a worthy member of the Methodist Church.

8 September 1831

Departed this life on Thursday, the 18th of August last, in Hall county, JOHN EBERHARDT, Esq. For two years he had been an orderly member of the Presbyterian Church.

22 September 1831

Died on the 18th inst. at the residence of Mrs. Ellis, in Baldwin county, JOSEPH STILES, youngest son of JOHN A. CUTHBERT, Esq., aged 23 months. Died at the Indian Springs on the 27th ult. ROBIN JACKSON, only son of COL. JOEL BAILY of that place.

20 October 1831

Died on Friday evening last of a lingering illness, MR. JOHN P. CHEELY, formerly of Brunswick county, Virginia, but for the last three years a citizen of this place, aged 24 years.

Died on Monday last at Sandersville, Washington county, REUBEN B. BARNEY. In the same county, last week, CAPT. REUBEN N. BICKLIN.

27 October 1831

Died on the evening of Tuesday last, after a protracted illness, at his residence in Jones county, DANIEL BOURDEAUX JUHAN, in the 33d year of his age - a native of the state of South Carolina, and for the last four years, a citizen of Jones county, Georgia.

Died at Lincolnton, Georgia on the 22d ultimo, DR. AZA BEALL, in the 37th year of his age.

Died in Camden county on the 14th instant, in the 19th year of her age, MRS. ISABELLA MELINDA HOPKINS, wife of Major Wm. P. Hopkins, of Darien, and youngest daughter of Gen. John Floyd.

3 November 1831

Died on the 22d day of September last, at his father's residence, 2 miles north of Decatur, DeKalb county, JAMES R. DICKSON, eldest son of Mr. Wm. Dickson of this county. Was 22 years 5 months and 25 days old; had been engaged for the last twenty months in the study of Medicine; was member of a literary institution in Decatur. (with Tribute of Respect)

10 November 1831

Died on the 6th instant, EDARDS BROWN, aged eighty years, a native of Luningburg county, Virginia, but for the last 40 years of his life a citizen of Georgia.

6

17 November 1831

Died on the 7th instant, in the 65th year of her age, after a short but severe illness, MRS. LUCINDA BETTON, consort of Capt. S. Betton of this place; twenty-six years membership in the Church of Christ.

Died on Wednesday the 26th of October, at his residence in Oglethorpe county, JOHN LUMPKIN, Esq., a soldier of the Revolution, aged 76 years - the father of our worthy Governor.

8 December 1831

Another Revolutionary Soldier gone. Departed this life on the first day of November, in the county of Wilkes, JOSEPH JOHNSON, Sen'r, aged ninety-eight. He was a native of the state of Virginia - and fought at the battle of Brandy wine.

29 December 1831

Died in this place on the 20th instant, JOSEPH T. WILLIAMS, aged 5 months and 17 days, son of NOBLE A. and MARTHA J. HARDIE, of Camden county, Georgia.

12 January 1832

Died at Fort Hill on the 23d ultimo, CHARLES PRICE, late of Wilkinson county, Ga., aged about 46 years. He was a native of South Carolina, and removed to this State about 20 years ago - during which time he was an exemplary member of the Methodist Episcopal Church.

26 January 1832

Died on the 6th instant at her late residence in this county, MRS. NANCY GREENE, consort of Rev. Miles Greene, in the 53d year of her age. Twenty five years of her life she had been a professor of religion in the Methodist Episcopal Church.

2 February 1832

Died on the 25th ult. MR. JOHN W. PITT, in the 45th year of his age - for several years a respectable citizen of this place.

A melancholy affair. A very serious meeting took place on monday the 23d inst. at Fort Mitchell, near this place, between GEN. SOWELL WOOLFOLK and Maj. Jos. T. Camp, both citizens of Columbus, in which the former was shot dead at the first fire, and the latter seriously, though not dangerously, wounded... (Democrat)

23 February 1832

Departed this life on the 6th inst. MR. MARCUS ANDREWS, at his residence near Crawfordville. Mr. Andrews was snatched off in the prime of life. He was seized with a severe affliction last fall, which terminated in the dropsy...member of Baptist Church.

1 March 1832

Died on the 11th ultimo, after an illness of six days, MRS. MARY BLACKBURN, consort of Daniel J. Blackburn, Esq., of Ware county, Georgia. For about 22 years she was an acceptable member of the Methodist Church; left an affectionate husband and six children (one a daughter married); she was the daughter of William Miller Esq. a native of North Carolina, a Revolutionary Soldier, who still remains in the land of the living.

Died at his residence in Pulaski county on the 14th inst. MR JAMES
BRACEWELL, in the 66th year of his age; he was a native of Edgecombe
county, N. Carolina, but for the last 27 years a citizen of this State.

22 March 1832

Died suddenly in this place on Saturday morning last, MR. JOHN SMITH,
aged twenty-one years, son of John R. Smith, Esq. of this county.

29 March 1832

Died at the residence of his son, Daniel W. Shine, in Twiggs county, on
Saturday, 11th March, after an illness of ten days, MR. JOHN SHINE, in
the 73d year of his age. The deceased was born in Jones county, North
Carolina, in 1759, and devoted a part of his youth to the service of his
country in the revolutionary war, under the command of General Caswell, and
was at the battle near Camden, S.C. in 1780; leaves children, grandchildren
and great-grandchildren (with eulogy).

Died at the seat of Hugh Lawson, in Houston county, on the 22nd March,
after a confining illness of three months, ROBERT GLENN, Esq. in the 57th
year of his age. Represented Twiggs county several years in the State
legislature.

5 April 1832

Died at his residence in Houston county on the morning of the 13th ult.,
of the epidemic influenza, CAPT. ABNER VEASEY, formerly of Putnam county,
aged 56 years. Volunteered and followed Gen. Jackson in the Seminole
campaign in the capacity of Captain. (with eulogy)

Died in Monroe county on Tuesday the 25th of March last, MR. JEPTHA HILL,
a useful and respectable citizen. Had left a family.

26 April 1832

COL. ZACHARIAH PHILLIPS died at Newnan on the morning of the 31st March, of
a pulmonary disease, in the 45th year of his age; member of Burns Lodge No. 27.
(with Tribute of Respect)

Departed this life on the 15th inst. at his residence in Randolph county,
after an illness of twenty two days, WILLIAM EVERETT, Esq., in the 29th
year of his age; leaves a wife and large circle of relatives; at time of
death was the Senator of that county in the State legislature, which station
he had filled for several years.

Died in DeKalb county on the 4th of March last, SARAH LAWSON, widow of
James Lawson, deceased.

Died in Pulaski county on Wednesday night the 11th inst. MR. DUNCAN L.C.
BRACEWELL, in his 22d year. Was son of the late James Bracewell of the
same place.

3 May 1832

Died in Hartford on the 28th April, MRS. MARTHA J. BRACEWELL, in the 23d
year of her age.

Died in Greensborough on the 22nd April, MRS. CHARITY GRIMES, Consort of
Thomas W. Grimes, Esq.

Fatal accident on afternoon of the tenth day of April inst. in
which LITTLETON P. McKAY, who resided near Covington, Newton county,
was killed...was 45 years of age (details of accident and with eulogy)

17 May 1832

Died in Savannah on Wedensday evening last, MR. THOMAS CORMICK, aged about
40 years, a native of Ireland.

Died on Tuesday the 1st inst. at the residence of her father (Mr. Henry
Greenwood) in Richmond county, MRS. MARY ANN PORTER, the wife of
Col. John S. Porter, of Baker county, aged 21 years and 9 days; leaves husband
and three infant children, her father and mother, and many relations and
friends to mourn her early exit from time to eternity. About the same time,
probably on the same day, COL. JOHN S. PORTER, of Baker county, died
suddenly at Hawkinsville, on his way home from North Carolina. He represented
the county in which he lived for several years in the Senate of the State.
He passed through Hartford on Friday in fine health - and a few miles beyond
Hawkinsville was taken suddenly ill - returned to that place, and on Monday
or Tuesday, after his physicians believed him out of danger, he died suddenly
and alone in his room.

14 June 1832

Died in Milledgeville on SATURDAY morning the 9th of June, MRS. ELIZABETH
SCOTT, aged 33 years, wife of Major William F. Scott.

Died at Savannah on the 2d instant, DR. L. H. FURTH, a native of Germany,
but for the last 16 years a resident of Savannah. His death was caused from
his attempting to reach the shore from a steamboat on a plank, only one end
of which was secured. His body lay in the water for more than two hours
before it was recovered. He has left a widow and six small children.

26 July 1832

Departed this life on Friday the 20th inst. at the residence of Mr. William
Schurlock near this place, the REV. S.B. TOWNSEND of the Presbyterian Church.
Was a native of Rhode Island, but had for several years before he left the
North laboured in the ministry in the State of Massachusetts, until his
health becoming much impaired by the ravages of disease, he sought his relief
in a milder climate. He visited St. Augustine where he lost his wife. When
death arrested his further progress he was on his way to the upper part of
this State.

2 August 1832

Died in Jackson, Butts county, on the 28th (?) July, after a lingering
illness of three months, HELEN JANE, daughter of THOMAS RAGLAND, of this place,
in the nineteenth month of her age.

16 August 1832

Died in this place on Friday the 10th inst. after an illness of two days,
BENJAMIN RANDOLPH, only son of JAMES G. and CHRISTINA S. SMITH, aged 2 years
2 months and 28 days.

Died in Hawkinsville on the 5th inst. FLOYD CROCKETT, infant son of JAMES
and MARTHA POLHILL.

23 August 1832
   Died near this place on the 14th instant, JAMES WILLIAM, youngest son
   of the REV. MYLES GREENE, aged 12 years and 28 days. (short eulogy)

30 August 1832
   Notice of the sudden death of MRS. ELIZABETH JANE GREENE, second daughter
   of Mr. James Stanford of this town; was married not twelve months since;
   leaves husband and infant child; in her 14th year she gave herself to the
   Church. (with eulogy)

13 September 1832
   Died in this place on the 11th inst. in the 68th year of her age,
   MRS. JUDITH HILL - member of the Baptist Church upwards of 40 years.

20 September 1832
   Died on the 16th inst. at Milledgeville, CAPT. SOLOMON BETTON, in the 73d
   year of his age. He was a soldier of the revolution.

   Died in Milledgeville on the 6th inst., of a painful and protracted illness,
   MRS. SUSAN T. KNOX, wife of Mr. H. Knox, in the 27th year of her age.

   Departed this life in Cullodenville, on Wednesday 22d inst., THERILIUS
   ALBERTUS, only son of COL. RICHARD BAILEY, of Upson county.

4 October 1832
. Died in Hawkinsville on Saturday the 22d September, MR. GEORGE W. COE,
   a merchant of Savannah.

11 October 1832
   Died on Thursday the 4th inst. at his late residence in Walton county,
   of a lingering illness, COL. VINCENT HARALSON, Clerk of the Superior and
   Inferior Courts of that county. From the first organization of the county,
   to his decease, he held those offices.

25 October 1832
   Died in this place on Monday the 8th instant MRS. NANCY LAMAR, consort of
   Dr. Thomas R. Lamar. (Macon Mess.)

   Died at the residence of her only child, Col. George Walton, of Pensacola,
   on the 12th of September last, MRS. DOROTHY WALTON, relict of the Hon. George
   Walton, one of the signers of the Declaration of Independence, and for
   several years one of the Judges of the Superior Court of the State of Georgia.
   Was for many years a resident of Augusta...three months after her marriage
   she was called to attend upon her husband, a prisoner and desperately wounded
   at the attack on Savannah. Shortly after his recovery, she was herself conveyed
   as a prisoner to the West Indies, and upon her return from imprisonment,
   suffered extremely from exposure to the rigors of winter, in an open boat.
   (Constitutionalist)

   Died in Augusta on the 10th inst. after a lingering illness, MR. DANIEL
   BRUCKNER, in the 67th year of his age. Had long been a resident of this
   place and was formerly editor of this paper. (Washington News)

15 November 1832
   Died on the 10th October last, at their residence in Washington county,
   MR. NATHANIEL and MRS. MARY STEWART.

6 December 1832

Died in Milledgeville on the 6th instant of typhus fever which he bore with manly firmness for fifteen days, MR. HORACE STEDMAN, aged 23 years. He was a native of Berlin, Conn., but had resided in this place for the last three years of his life.

(From the Savannah Georgian, Nov. 27). COL. EDWARD F. TATTNALL departed this life on the morning of the 21st inst. in the 42 year of his age, was born at Bonaventure, the family seat of his ancestors, near this city...

Died suddenly yesterday at 6 o'clock P.M., the Hon. PHILIP DODDRIDGE, member of Congress from Virginia. (Washington Globe, Nov. 20)

13 December 1832

Died in Gadsden county, Florida on the 8th ult. RICHARD MORGAN, Esq., a native of Dublin, Ireland, and formerly a citizen of Milledgeville.

Died at Montgomery, Alabama on the 28th ult. NAPOLEON P. BATES, son of Gen. John Bates, of Hall county, Ga. Had recently settled in Montgomery, and was only in his nineteenth year.

20 December 1832

Departed this life at his residence in Dooly county on Sunday 2d inst., Major JAMES C. BRYAN, in the 58th year of his age. Was a native of North Carolina; In that State he had conferred upon him many appointments both civil and military; represented Jones county for ten years; emigrated to this State in 1814 and settled in Hartford, Pulaski county. (with eulogy)

27 December 1832

Died in this place on the night of the 23d inst. the REV. THOMAS RHODES, of Jasper county; member of Baptist Church and a Minister of the Gospel; at the time of his death, he was a Commissioner of the Land Lottery now in progress, and was in the discharge of his duties in that office, when he was taken with a violent cold which settled on his lungs, and produced his death.

10 January 1833

Died in Milledgeville on Monday the 24th of December last of spasmodic asthma, the REV. THOMAS RHODES, in the 61st year of his age; pious member of the Baptist Church nearly forty years.

7 February 1833

Died on Friday the 1st inst. at Mount Ariel, in Washington county, WILLIAM A. SKRINE, Esq. in the 31st year of his age; left a widow and four children.

Died at Macon on the 1st ult. MRS. ELIZABETH ERWIN, wife of Leander A. Erwin, Esq. formerly of Athens.

Died after a lingering illness of nearly twelve months, in Jackson county, west Florida, on the 8th of January last, MR. FARISH CARTER WALKER, in the 24th year of his age.

21 February 1833

Died at his residence near Bethlehem, Jasper county, on Thursday 7th inst., in the 60th year of his age, STOKELY MORGAN, Esq. Mr. Morgan never made a profession of the Christian religion, though his wife and two eldest daughters are useful members of the Baptist Church of Bethlehem. He was a decided friend of all religious institutions, such as Missionary, Bible, Tract, and Sunday School Societies, and contributed liberally to their support. Was a member of the Masonic fraternity. His funeral will be preached from his former residence on the fifth Sabbath in March next, by the Rev. Cyrus White.

Died in Newnan on the 10th inst. , JOHN GILCHRIST, a native of Scotland, but for many years past a resident of Georgia; a member of Burns Lodge 27. (with eulogy)

28 February 1833

Died suddenly on Sunday morning the 24th instant, at his residence in Butts county, MICAJAH FERRELL, at about the age of seventy-five years. In his youth, he was devoted to the service of his country. first as a soldier, and afterwards as an officer in the Revolutionary War.

14 March 1833

Died on Wednesday the 27th February last, near Irwinton, Wilkinson county, THOMAS GRAY, a revolutionary soldier, in the 81st year of his age; member of the Baptist Church; left an aged relict (who soon must follow him).

Died on Wednesday the 27th of February, after an illness of twenty days, MRS. JANE WALKER, wife of Jonathan Walker, Esq. of Carroll county, aged about 40 years; leaves husband and six children; has been from her youth an acceptable member of the Baptist Church. (with eulogy)

Died in Savannah on Friday, the 15th of February, MRS. MISSISSIPPI CUYLER, wife of Richard R. Cuyler, aged 33 years. (short eulogy)

Died at his residence near Waynesborough, Burke county, on the morning of the 23d ult. after an illness of 11 days, DR. SOUTHWORTH HARLOW, aged 53 years. Leaves wife and three children.

11 April 1833

Died in Milledgeville on the 7th instant, MR. DENIS MAHONEY, formerly of Lincoln county, Ga., aged about forty-five years.

Died in Milledgeville on the 6th instant, ANN ELIZABETH FORT, youngest child of Dr. Tomlinson Fort, aged 19 months and 3 days.

2 May 1833

Died on the 31st March last in Gwinnett county, Ga., MRS. MARY ANN BLACKMAN, of Talbot county, after an extreme illness of twenty days; leaves three children.

23 May 1833

Died on the 6th inst. MRS. EMILY JACKSON, consort of Albertus E. Jackson, of Meriwether county, and youngest daughter of Capt. William Saunders, deceased, of Hancock county, aged 21 years and 7 months; member of the Methodist Church; leaves a husband, an only child, a doating mother, and many relations and friends to mourn their loss.

13 June 1833

Departed this life, the venerable patriot, OLIVER WOLCOTT, in the 74th year of his age. He was Secretary of the Treasury under President Washington, and afterwards Governor of Connecticut.

11 July 1833

Died in Augusta on Saturday the 29th ult. of the dropsy, patiently borne for six months, MATHEW WILLIAM COOPER, (son of Wm. Cooper, deceased) aged 5 years and 7 months.

25 July 1833

Died on the 12th instant in Talbot county, at the residence of his Father-in-law, MR. WILSON HOGAN, formerly of Twiggs county, in the 27th year of his age.

1 August 1833

Died at the residence of Mrs. July Neely, in Washington county, on the 16th ultimo, JOHN STANTON, in the 94th year of his age. He held the rank of Captain during the Revolutionary War, was engaged in several battles, and was present at the capture of Cornwallis. He died from old age; was born in North Carolina (Northampton County), but for the last thirty years has been a citizen of this State.

Died in Jones county, Ga. on the 28th June, MRS. SARAH T. TAYLOR, consort of Swepson Taylor, aged 32 years 2 months and 21 days; member of the Methodist Episcopal Church. (with long eulogy)

8 August 1833

Died in Hamilton, Harris county, Ga. on the 31st ult. THOMAS JEFFERSON NIX, the son of Joseph and Mahaley Nix, aged 19 months and 2 days.

Died at Philadelphia on the 27th ult. Commodore WILLIAM BAINBRIDGE, of the United States navy, a native of Princeton, New Jersey, in the 60th year of his age...

15 August 1833

Died at the residence of Mr. Jacob P. Turner, within two miles of Milledgeville, on the evening of the 10th instant, MR. ROBERT MACKAY, a native of Cromartie, in the Highlands of Scotland, about 32 years of age. (Died in accident while sinking a well). Funeral was preached in Methodist Church in Milledgeville; had left Scotland five or six years ago, but at the time of his death had resided in Georgia only a few months.

Died on the 28th ult. after a short illness, in Camden county, Ga., ANN ELIZA, daughter of MARTHA T. and NOBLE A. HARDEE, aged 5 years and 3 months. At the time of the child's demise, her mother, who was in a very delicate situation, became so much affected at the hopeless condition of her only surviving child, that she was attacked with a severe illness, and on the 3d inst. she sank to rest, the victim of puerperal fever, aged 21 years and 3 months. (with eulogy)

22 August 1833

Died of scarlet fever at the residence of Dr. Pleasant Philips, in Jones county, Ga. on the 15th instant, AMANDA MINERVA PHILIPS, (eldest daughter of Dr. Pleasant Philips) aged 12 years and 8 months. She was sick only three days.

Died in Newbern, North Carolina on the 3d instant, the Hon. JOHN STANLY...

Died of spasmodic cholera, at his residence in Belleville, State of Illinois, on the 20th ult., the Hon. NINIAN EDWARDS, late Governor of Illinois...

12 September 1833

Departed this life on the 2d instant, MRS. NANCY D. ROBERTS, consort of Mr. William M. Roberts, of Jasper county, aged 33 years, after a long and tedious affliction: leaves husband and three small children (with long eulogy)

16 October 1833

Departed this life on the evening of the 12th inst. at the house of Dr. White, in this place. JAMES MERCER, son of MR. JAMES G. SALISBURY, of Randolph county, aged 12 months and 14 days.

30 October 1833

Died at his residence in Twiggs county on the 19th inst. ARTHUR FORT, in the 85th year of his age. He has been a resident and citizen of Georgia for 75 years - a soldier and statesman of the revolution, a member of the committee of safety in the darkest hour of the revolution.

Died at Macdonough, Henry county, Ga. on the 12th instant, MRS. MARY ANN MINER, (wife of Samuel Wright Miner, Esq. editor of the Macdonough Jacksonian) aged 46 years. Her disease was a rose-cancer on her left breast, and under her left shoulder. (The Huntsville Republican and Centreville Times are requested to insert the above for the information of Mrs. Miner's relations).

20 November 1833

Died in Talbotton, Talbot county, Ga. on the 11th instant, JOHN G., son of CHARLES R. and ELIZABETH WYNNE, aged 4 years and 17 days.

Died on the evening of the 11th inst. in Coweta county, Ga. MRS. ANN B. (consort of HENRY KELLER Esq. late sheriff of Coweta county, and only daughter of William M. Stokes Esq.) aged 24 years and 9 days - leaving an infant nine days old.

27 November 1833

Died on Sunday morning 17th instant, at the residence of his son Benjamin, the venerable COL. THOMAS TAYLOR, the founder of Columbia, and one of the honored actors in that eventful revolution which has secured liberty to twelve millions of the human family...

4 December 1833

Died in Charleston, South Carolina, on the 26th ultimo, Major JAMES HAMILTON Sen. (the father of General Hamilton) the oldest surviving officer of the Continental Army of the Revolutionary War. aged 83 years.

11 December 1833

Died at West Point, Troup county, on the 1st instant, MR. PHILIP N. GILDER (a merchant of that place) aged 27 years 7 months and 19 days.

Died at his residence in South Carolina on the 14th ultimo, after a painful illness of fourteen days, JOHN DAVID MONGIN, one of the last of the revolutionary worthies, aged 71 years and 11 months.

1 January 1834

Died lately at his residence in Madison, Morgan county, Major EDWARD MEAD, aged 22 years 8 months 20 days; leaves a widow and two orphans.

15 January 1834

Another Revolutionary Soldier is gone! Died on the 3d instant at his late residence in Monroe county, MATHEW DUNHAM, aged 74 years; for more than fifty years preceding his death an honored member of the Baptist Church.

22 January 1834

Died on the 14th inst. ANN ELIZABETH, youngest daughter of WM. F. SCOTT, aged 2 years 2 months and 18 days; died of scarlet fever.

5 February 1834

Died at his residence in Jones county, on the 30th ultimo, WILLIAM HUNT, (the father of the Junior Editor of the Federal Union) a native of Virginia, in the 63rd year of his age.

12 February 1834

Died at her residence near Forsyth, Monroe county, MRS. MARY WATSON, in the 76th year of her age; for many years a worthy member of the Presbyterian Church.

19 February 1834

Another Revolutionary Soldier gone! Died on the 17th inst. (February 1834) at Milledgeville, JAMES DUNCAN, Senior, aged 82 years and 13 days. He was a native of Virginia, and entered the army of his country at the commencement of the revolutionary war.

Died at his residence in Baldwin county, on the 14th of January last, CORNELIUS MURPHY, aged 64 years.

Died on the 6th inst. at his residence near Marion, Twiggs county. MR. MESSICK EASON, in the 48th year of his age.

Died at his residence in Butts county on the 31st ultimo, JOHN R. CARGILE, Esq. aged 40 years; represented Butts in the senatorial branch of the Legislature.   (with eulogy)

26 February 1834

Died on the 12th inst. in Gwinnett county after a painful confinement of many months (from cancer in the breast), MRS. SARAH BETTS, wife of Elisha Betts, Esq. and sister of Col. Mills of Milledgeville, aged about 47 years. Member of the Baptist Church; had no children. For the information of the relatives of the deceased at a distance, notice is given that her funeral will be preached at Bethel, near Warsaw, Gwinnett county on the fifth Sabbath of March next.

5 March 1834

    Died at his residence in Coweta county, Ga. on Wednesday the 26th ultimo, ANDREW BROWN, Esq., formerly a resident of Walton county, aged 39 years - leaving a widow and nine children.

    Departed this life on the 14th ult. in the 32d year of her age, MRS. MARTHA DANIELL, daughter of the late Major John Screven, and wife of Dr. W.C. Daniell, of Savannah. (Savannah Republican)

    Died, about meridian, on the 18th February, in Washington city, WILLIAM WIRT Esq. aged about 62 years. (long eulogy) (National Intelligencer)

19 March 1834

    Died in Augusta on the 6th instant, the venerable THOMAS CUMMING. (with eulogy)

2 April 1834

    Died of typhus fever at the residence of her husband in Henry county, on the morning of the 11th ult., MRS. ELIZABETH POPE, consort of Henry N. Pope, Esq., in the 38th year of her age. (short eulogy)

16 April 1834

    Died on the 16th ult. at Lagrange, Troup county, Georgia, MR. THOS. G. ALLEN, in the 28th year of his age. Returning from a journey of twelve months' absence at the North, apparently in perfect health, he was attacked by disease when within a few miles of the abode of his relatives, and in fifteen days breathed his last, to join in heaven, it is believed, his father and sister who died a few years ago.

    Died in Perry, Houston county, on Sunday morning, 6th inst. the Rev. ROBERT FLOURNOY, aged 37 years; able and eloquent minister of the Methodist Episcopal Church. (with long eulogy)

30 April 1834

    Another Revolutionary Soldier departed! Died on the 10th day of April 1834, at his residence in the county of Monroe, ABRAHAM WOMACK, in the 91st year of his age.

7 May 1834

    Died in Jasper county, Ga. on the 12th instant, SOLOMON WALDREP, in the 63d year of his age. For the last thirty years of his life he was an exemplary member of the Baptist Church; leaves widow and numerous relations.

    Died suddenly in Union District, South Carolina, on the 16th ult. General E. DAWKINS, of that district.

14 May 1834

    Died in Milledgeville on the 25th ult. of pulmonary consumption, in the 26th year of his age, DANIEL BARRINGER, a native of North Carolina, but for the last four or five years a resident of this place.

    Died at Darien on the 18th ult. after a long and lingering illness, MARCUS T. PIERCE Esq. in the 34th year of his age, leaving a disconsolate widow and one child to lament his premature death.

28 May 1834

Died in Henry county on the 10th instant, MRS. CHARLOTTE JONES MOSELEY, consort of Mr. Henry Moseley, in the 20th year of her age, and by a singular and melancholly coincidence, her younger brother NORBORN POWELL FAULKNER, son of Mr. Zachariah Faulkner, of Jasper county, who was on a visit to his sister's at the time, and after a brief illness, and on the same day likewise expired in the seventh year of his age.

Died in Jones county, Ga. after a protracted illness, on the evening of the 5th instant, MRS. JULIET A. JOURDAN, consort of Colonel Warren Jourdan, aged 34 years. Leaves an afflicted husband and three small daughters.

Died at his late residence in Bedford county, Tennessee,on the 19th ultimo, Colonel ANDREW ERWIN, in the 61st year of his age.

Died in Middleton, Connecticut, on the 21st ultimo, MR. THOMAS HOBBY, in the 60th year of his age.

11 June 1834

Died in Jasper county, Ga. on the 15th ultimo, JOHN B. SLAUGHTER, Esq. aged 33 years. At the January election preceding his death, the people of Jasper, knowing his worth, elected him to the office of sheriff of their county; leaves a widow and several helpless orphans. (short eulogy)

18 June 1834

Died of fever on the 29th ultimo, at the residence of his father, near the Peachstone Shoals, in Henry county, Georgia, MR. HENRY H. MOSELY, in the 22d year of his age. Mr. Mosely was the husband of an affectionate wife, whom it was the will and pleasure of God to call from time to eternity only a few days before his death. (short eulogy)

Major JOHN H. WALKER is no more. He died on Sunday the 8th instant of the consumption, aged 29 years. The Major left his residence a week previous, for Florida, and alas! never returned. He died at General Irwin's, in Alabama, in one short hour after he reached there, four miles only from Fort Gaines, his home. His remains were interred in the cemetery at this place the next day. Has left an only son and a bereaved widow. (Fort Gaines, June 11, 1834)

25 June 1834

Died in Savannah on the 2d instant, JOHN H. MOREL, Esq. late United States Marshal for the district of Georgia, in the 54th year of his age.

Died in Augusta on the 11th instant, MR. CHARLES WILLIAMSON, formerly of Milledgeville, in the 60th year of his age.

2 July 1834

Died at the residence of Thomas Liddell Esq. in Jackson county, Georgia, on the 12th ult. after a protracted and painful illness, MRS. ESTHER HEMPHILL, relict of Jonathan Hemphill Esq. late of said county; a professor in the Presbyterian Church.

9 July 1834

Died in Burke county, near Waynesborough, of a cramp in the stomach, MR. JEREMIAH BURK, aged 28 years - leaving an affectionate wife and two children to mourn their loss.

16 July 1834

Died at Talbotton on the 10th instant, CHARLES L. PACE, Esq., Attorney at Law, and a distinguished member of the last Legislature, from the county of Talbot.

Died at Columbus on the 11th instant, GEORGE C. SHIVERS, Esq., Attorney at Law, of that city.

Died at Athens, Ga. on the 5th instant, MRS. PENELOPE NISBET,(relict of the late Dr. James Nisbet) a native of Henry county, Virginia, but for the last forty years a resident of Georgia, aged 58 years; leaves a numerous family of children.

23 July 1834

Died on Saturday the 12th inst. at the residence of Mrs. Thomas Cumming, on the Sand-hills near Augusta, MRS. SARAH G. CUTHBERT, wife of Alfred Cuthbert, Esq. of Jasper county, Ga.

6 August 1834

Died in Twiggs county, Ga. on the 27th ultimo, MRS. BERSHEBA WHEELER, consort of Noah Wheeler, aged 44 years; for 16 or 17 years an accepted member of the Baptist Church; left a husband and two daughters.

13 August 1834

Died at the residence of his mother in Iredell county, North Carolina on the 28th of July, Colonel FINLEY G. STEWART, late of Fayetteville, Georgia.

Died at Gainesville, Hall county, on Monday the 28th ult. MR. JAMES A. JOHNSTON, in the 31st year of his age; was attacked by bilious fever and inflammation of the stomach; he died on the sixth day. (short eulogy)

27 August 1834

Died at Columbus, Ga. on the 20th instant, GEORGE W. DILLINGHAM Esq., formerly of Lee, Berkshire county, Massachusetts, but for several years past merchant of Columbus, in the 31st year of his age.

10 September 1834

Died on the 4th inst. in the 57th year of his age, at his residence near Eatonton, Putnam county, Ga., the Rev. JOHN COLLINSWORTH, an itinerant minister of the Methodist Episcopal Church. He embraced religion in the thirteenth year of his age. (with eulogy)

Died on the 27th of August 1834 in Jones county, Ga., MRS. LUCY COOK, aged 49 years; for 35 years a reputable member of the Methodist Church; newspapers in the Southwestern States are requested to publish the foregoing obituary notice, for the information of William Cook, her absent husband, who is believed to be in one of those states.

Died at his residence in Walton county on the 18th ult., MR. NATHAN FORMBY, aged 74 years and 4 days - an active soldier in the Revolutionary War; lived 56 years a member of the Baptist Church; leaves an aged widow and children.

24 September 1834

Died in Scottsborough, near Milledgeville, on the 3d instant, MR. JAMES BOZEMAN, a native of North Carolina, aged 60 years.

Died in Macon on the 14th instant, MRS. SUSAN C. TRACY (consort of Edward D. Tracy, Esq.), in the 26th year of her age.

1 October 1834

Died on the 5th ult. at the house on Andrew Weldon in Jasper county, Ga., ABRAHAM RIDDICK, aged 94 years. The deceased was a soldier of the Revolutionary War.

15 October 1834

Died at Lexington, Mississippi on the 28th of August last, DR. TERRELL H. JONES, aged 24 years and 10 months. Was a native of Carnesville, Georgia. Graduated at Transylvalia University in March 1833. Early last winter he married an amiable young lady of his native county, a daughter of major John Bush, of Franklin county. Last spring, with hopes elate and spirits buoyant, he badefarewell to his widowed mother, brothers and sisters and friends, and sped his way to the far west, in pursuit of fortune and fame... (with long eulogy)

29 October 1834

Died on the 19th instant, General DAVID ADAMS, of Jasper county, Ga. in the 69th year of his age.

Died on the 14th instant in Marion, Twiggs county, Ga., Colonel SEABORN DELK.

Died suddenly on the 17th instant at his residence in Wilkinson county, Ga., MR. MARTIN WIT, aged 56 years.

(From The Charleston Observer, 25th instant) - death of REV. THOMAS S. GRIMKE. He fell victim to the cholera in Columbus (Ohio). (long eulogy)

5 November 1834

Died in Milledgeville, Georgia on the 28th ultimo, THOMAS GOULDING, second son of JOHN A. and LOUISA E. CUTHBERT, aged 7 years and 2 months.

Died on the 29th instant GEORGIANA VIRGINIA, infant daughter of PRYOR and MARGARET S. WRIGHT, aged 9 months and 25 days.

Died in Milledgeville on the 29th of October, Col. ZACHARIAH LAMAR, in the 66th year of his age. In early life, he bore arms in the cause of his country; and in his mature years, he had a seat in her legislative bodies.

Died at his residence in Jones county, Georgia on the 29th ultimo, MR. BENJAMIN REYNOLDS, aged 73 years; a native of Caroline county, Virginia; soldier of Rev. War; at end of war he removed to South Carolina into a neighborhood distinguished for their loyalty to the British Crown; he encountered the most violent opposition from his misguided associated that he removed to Jones county and was one of its earliest residents.

19 November 1834

Died in Meriwether county on the 10th instant, MRS. ANN WOOD, consort of Mr. Stephen Wood. Mrs. Wood was born 22d September 1793, and she was married to Mr. Wood on 2d March 1826; has left a husband and five small children.

Died in Twiggs county on the 6th instant, at sunrise, HALLIDAY H. HARROLL. (short eulogy)

Died in Monroe county on the 5th instant, MARY ANN, daughter of JOHN SHOCKLEY, ESQUIRE, aged 10 years 10 months 18 days. She was afflicted for 23 days with bilious fever. (with eulogy)

26 November 1834

Died in Baldwin county on the 23d instant, MR. ELI LESTER, aged 44 years; for several years an exemplary member of the Baptist Church.

Died in Columbus on the 19th instant, MRS. ELIZA WATSON, consort of General James C. Watson, in the 39th year of her age. (short eulogy)

Died on the 5th instant at her father's (Colonel John Mills' residence) in Rutherford county, North Carolina, MRS. HARRIET CAMP, consort of the late Major Joseph T. Camp of Columbus; leaves two small children.

3 December 1834

Died on Saturday the 15th ultimo in Baldwin county, MRS. AMEY MYRICK, consort of Mr. John Myrick, in the 85th year of her age; an acceptable member of the Methodist Episcopal Church for 45 years; for the last ten years confined by sore affliction; has left an aged husband with whom she has lived in the bonds of union for sixty years.

Died at the seat of government on the 25th ultimo, the Honorable JONATHAN LEWIS, senator from the county of Burke. In token respect for his memory, both branches of the general assembly adjourned on the 26th, as soon as they were informed of his decease.

10 December 1834

Died in this place on the night of the 11th instant, McLIN LUNDAY, Esq. a representative from the county of Screven.

Died on the evening of the 5th instant in this place, MRS. ELIZA BROWN, consort of Dr. George A. Brown.

Died at the residence of his father in Forsyth, Monroe county, Ga. on the evening of the 5th instant, MR. COLEMAN P. NALL, in the 22d year of his age. (with eulogy)

17 December 1834

Died in Greene county on the 9th instant, MRS. SARAH JACKSON, wife of Moses Jackson jr. after a lingering illness of ten weeks.

31 December 1834

Died in Milledgeville on the 30th instant, in the 36th year of his age, DRURY MURPHY, Esq. a highly respected citizen of this place. His disease was pulmonary consumption.

Died of pulmonary consumption on the 21st instant at the residence of his widowed mother, in Macon, Doctor LOUIS JEFFERSON WILLIAMSON KRAATZ.

20 January 1835

Died at her residence in Morgan county on the 17th November last,after a severe illness of eight days, MRS. NANCY SHEPHERD, consort of James Shepherd, in the 51st year of her age. (short eulogy)

27 January 1835

Died at his residence in Sumter county on the 12th instant, MR. MOSES SHELBY, in the 47th year of his age; an exemplary member of the Methodist Episcopal Church for four years previous to his death.

Died in Savannah on the 10th instant, DR. MOSES SHEFTALL, one of the oldest and most respected natives of that city. His death was occasioned by an affection of the heart.

3 February 1835

Died on the evening of Saturday the 24th ultimo in Irwinton, Wilkinson county, MR. JOEL NEAL, aged 36 years. He was a native of Connecticut, but for the last five years a citizen of Georgia; leaves a wife and five orphans.

Another revolutionary hero gone - death of Major Hamilton of Abbeville. Died on the evening of the 17th ult. at his residence in Abbeville, ANDREW HAMILTON, in the 94th year of his age. Major Hamilton was born in Virginia and emigrated to this state some years previous to the revolution. At the surrender of Carns fort by the British, Major Hamilton was the officer selected by the commander of the American forces to negotiate the capitulation. At the battle of Eutaw, he was near Major Thomas Pinckney (the late Major Thomas Pinckney) when that meritorious officer was wounded...served for many years as a member of the legislature and was a member of the convention that adopted the constitution of the United States.

10 February 1835

Died at his residence in Washington county, Ga. on the 26th ultimo, MEISELS WOOD, in the 74th year of his age. Was a soldier of the revolutionary war in the cause of liberty.

17 February 1835

Died on the 4th instant at his residence in Columbia, South Carolina, General WADE HAMPTON, in the 81st year of his age.

Died on the 19th ultimo in Morgan county, WILLIAM B. STALLINGS, (son of Colonel William Stallings) aged 21 years; victim of consumption.

Died on the 6th instant in the town of Forsyth, Monroe county, MRS. SARAH M. BALDWIN (consort of Captain Anderson Baldwin), in the 28th year of her age; leaves husband and three children (long eulogy)

24 February 1835

Died at Elberton on the 1st instant, BENAJAH HOUSTON, Esq., formerly clerk of the superior court of said county.

Died in Macon on the 17th instant, MR. MARTIN SIMMONS, clerk of the inferior court of Bibb county.

3 March 1835

Died in Milledgeville, Ga. on the 26th ultimo, HENRY JAMES, eldest child of HENRY and ELIZABETH MANGUM, aged 2 years 9 months 4 days.

10 March 1835

Died in Harris county, Ga. on the 31st of January last, MRS. HARRIET BOWDRE BARNES, (consort of John Barnes, Esq.) in the 35th year of her age; for several years a member of the Methodist Episcopal Church.

17 March 1835

Died in Montgomery, Alabama on the 28th ultimo, MR. WILLIAM D. BUNKLEY, a native of Jones county, Ga. but for the last two years an inhabitant of Alabama, in the 24th year of his age.

31 March 1835

Died at Forsyth, Monroe county, Georgia on the 4th instant, MR. ISAAC P. EVANS, aged 23 years. (with long eulogy)

Died at Columbus, Georgia on the 14th instant, MRS. ANABELLA MARTIN, consort of Barkly Martin Esq. in the 51st year of her age.

Died in Talbotton, Talbot county, Georgia on the 12th instant, Colonel JOHN N. BIRCH, in the 40th year of his age; leaves a wife and several children. (short eulogy)

7 April 1835

Died in Milledgeville on the 2d instant, HENRY W. MALONE ESQ., late cashier of the Central Bank, in the 36th year of his age. His disease was pulmonary consumption; worthy member of the Methodist Episcopal Church.

Died on the 29th ult. in Talbot county, MRS. MARTHA BURKS, (consort of James L. Burks Esq.) in the 40th year of her age; pious and exemplary member of the Baptist Church for fifteen years; leaves husband and a large family.

21 April 1835

Died on the 11th instant at his residence in Greenville, Meriwether county, Ga., HUGH WALTON ECTOR, in the 37th year of his age. (eulogy)

28 April 1835

Dreadful tornado at Columbia, Tennessee. One of the most violent hurricanes ever witnessed in this State, passed over the lower part of this county on the night of the 21st March...persons killed included MR. FRANCIS G. DEGRAPHENREID, aged 21 years; JOHN DEGRAPHENREID, aged 14 years; T.L. DEGRAPHENREID, a child about 3 years of age; another infant about six weeks old of the same family; MR. ELIAS LUSK; MRS. LUSK; a MR. HILL; and a negro...

22

5 May 1835
   Died at his residence in Newton, Baker county, Ga. on the 19th
   ultimo, JOEL L. SCARBOROUGH Esq. in the 42d year of his age, after
   ten days sickness with the bilious pleurisy.

   Died in Butts county, Georgia on the 18th ultimo, MRS. NANCY BICKERSTOFF,
   (consort of Robert Bickerstoff) in the 52d year of her age; leaves
   husband; member of the Baptist Church (with eulogy)

   Departed this life on Thursday the 23rd ult. after a long and protracted
   illness, MR. THOMAS CROWELL, aged 48 years. (with eulogy)

12 May 1835
   Died at his residence in Wilkinson county, Georgia on the 20th ult.,
   Major JOHN HATCHER, in the 83rd year of his age - a patriotic and
   fearless soldier of the Revolution.

   Died in Warren county, Georgia on the 22d ultimo, Colonel ATHELSTAN
   ANDREWS, in the 35th year of his age.

   (From the Columbus Sentinel of the 7th inst.) -- JOHN ROBERT WATKINS CLARK,
   younger son of the late and much lamented Gen. John Clark, formerly of
   this state, breathed his last in the town of Milledgeville, in the 20th
   year of his age, at 4 o'clock P.M. on the 2d inst. (long eulogy)

26 May 1835
   Died in Monroe county on the 21st ult. MRS. DELILA REDDING, consort of
   Anderson Redding, sen. in the 67th year of her age; member of the
   Methodist Episcopal Church upwards of thirty years; leaves an aged
   husband, seven children, several grandchildren.

   Died on the 9th May (1835) after an illness of nearly four days,
   BENJAMIN HOLLAND Esq. of Randolph county, aged 40 years 10 months 14 days;
   leaves constant wife and an amiable daughter.

16 June 1835
   Died in Irwinton, Wilkinson county, Georgia on the 6th instant, Col.
   VALENTINE A. BRAZZILL, aged 37 years.

   Died on Friday morning the 29th ultimo, at his residence, Pleasant Grove,
   Henry county, SAMUEL JOHNSON Esq., formerly of Oglethorpe but for many
   years a worthy citizen of Henry; has left a very numerous family.

23 June 1835
   Died on Wednesday the 17th instant, SARAH F.H. DAVIS, infant daughter
   of Mrs. Emeline and William J. Davis, aged 21 months and 2 days.

   Died on the 26th of May last, MRS. CYNTHIA CRENSHAW, consort of Micajah
   Crenshaw, and mother of four interesting children, after a painful
   illness of three weeks. She was a member of the Baptist Church in
   Cuthbert, Randolph county. Her disease was inflammation of the lungs.

30 June 1835
   Died at his residence in Twiggs county, near Marion, Georgia, on the
   night of the 22nd inst., Major WILLIAM CROCKER, in the 58th year of
   his age; represented his citizens in the popular branch of the State
   Legislature. (long eulogy)

11 July 1835

Fatal encounter. On the evening of the 4th, a sudden quarrel arose in this place, which quickly terminated in the death of MARTIN P. SMITH by a pistol ball...

18 July 1835

Died on the evening of the 11th instant in the town of Hillsborough, Jasper county, Ga., JOHN C. EASTER, Adjutant General of the State of Georgia, in the 45th year of his age.

25 July 1835

Died at his residence in Jasper county on the 12th instant, THOMAS PHELPS, in the 77th year of his age; one of the few remaining soldiers of the revolution; a kind and affectionate husband and father; leaves a numerous family.

8 August 1835

Died in Milledgeville on the 29th July, in the 77th year of his age, after a painful illness of more than seven months, ROBERT B. WASHINGTON, senior, a native of Nottingham, England. He came to this country soon after the close of the Revolutionary War - was married, and settled in Wilkes county, Georgia - continuing a resident of that county until the year 1819, when he removed to Milledgeville, where he resided until his death; for more than thirty years a member of the Methodist Episcopal Church; leaves widow and children. (with long eulogy)

29 August 1835

Died in Baldwin county, Ga. on the 14th instant, after a short illness of twenty-four hours, MARY ANN, youngest daughter of EZEKIEL HARRIS, deceased, aged 8 years 7 months 20 days. (with eulogy)

Died at the residence of A.S. Rutherford, in Lumpkin county, on the 10th instant, of cholera morbus, ELIZABETH, aged 2 years 7 months and 27 days, youngest child of the late H.V. HOWARD of Columbus.

12 September 1835

Died at his late residence in Washington county, Georgia on the 25th day of August, after a short illness of six days, the Rev. JORDAN SMITH, aged 58 years 7 months 15 days; exemplary member of the Baptist Church nearly thirty years; has left a widow and eight children.

19 September 1835

Died in Milledgeville, Ga. on the 12th instant, ELIZABETH LANKTON, infant daughter of HUMPHREY and ELIZABETH MARTIN, aged 1 year and 7 months.

26 September 1835

Died on the 9th instant at Greenville, Meriwether county, Georgia, ELIZA JANE GRANT, daughter of Mrs. W.B. Ector, aged 14 years 3 months 2 days. Her disease was dropsy of the head and chest.

Died at the Sweet Springs in Monroe county, Virginia, DR. R.R. TARVER, of Twiggs county, Georgia, in the 40th year of his age; a native of Brunswick county, Virginia; emigrated to Georgia when just of age...

3 October 1835

Died at his residence in Morgan county, Georgia, of Bilious Fever, on the 29th ult. in the 63rd year of his age, JAMES SHEPHERD, one of the oldest and most respected citizens of that county.

24 October 1835

Died in Milledgeville, Ga. on the 20th instant, MR. HUMPHREY MARTIN, (printer) in the 29th year of his age - born in Dublin, Ireland, raised in Gibralter, Spain, and during the last eight years an inhabitant of the United States.

Died at Evansville, Morgan county, on Thursday the 15th instant of bilious fever, HEDGES T. CONGER, (Rector of the Evansville Academy, in the 24th year of his age.

Died at his residence in Monroe county, Ga. on the 7th instant, Major SINGLETON DURHAM.

Died in Athens on the 10th instant, MRS. ANN M'DONALD, wife of C.J. M'Donald, in the 35th year of her age; member of the Baptist Church (with eulogy)

6 November 1835

Died on Saturday the 24th ultimo in Putnam county, Ga., MRS. MARTHA ANN HARVEY, consort of Edmund C. Harvey and daughter of Charles Mathis and Mary Mathis, formerly of Hancock county; leaves husband and five children.

13 November 1835

Died at the residence of her father in Scottsborough, Baldwin county, Ga. on Sunday evening the 8th instant, MISS EMILY ADELINE, eldest daughter of Captain THOMAS GILBERT, aged 15 years an nearly 3 months. (short eulogy)

20 November 1835

Died in Wilcox county, Alabama on the 7th ult. the Honorable CHARLES TAIT, formerly member OF Congress and Judge of the Superior Court of this State, in the 68th year of his age.

27 November 1835

Died at Bellevue, Talbot county, Ga. on the 14th instant, after a painful and protracted illness, DR. SAMUEL H. BREWSTER, (of the Warm Springs, Meriwether county, Ga.) in the 23rd year of his age. (The Columbus Sentinel and Enquirer are requested to publish the above)

Died at his residence near Augusta, Ga. on the 14th instant, MR. JOSEPH EVE, in the 76th year of his age. He was (says the Augusta Constitutionalist) a native of Pennsylvania, where he was reared to manhood...early in life his fortunes led him to the West Indies, where he spent twenty years of a life of great industry and usefulness. On returning to the United States and after a residence of a few years in Carolina, he procured an humble home in this neighborhood, where he spent the rest of his days...

11 December 1835

Died in the county of Upson on the 12th of November, CAROLINE CASTLEN, daughter of John and Eliza Castlen.

Died on Saturday morning the 5th instant at the residence of her mother (Mrs. Martha Myrick) in Baldwin county, Ga., MRS. SARAH ADELINE McGEHEE, consort of Mr. Edmond McGehee, in the 17th year of her age; leaves a husband, infant son and widowed mother.

Died in Jones county, Georgia on the 1st instant, MRS. MARGA ANN REYNOLDS, in the 17th year of her age; leaves husband and infant son.

25 December 1835

Died in Milledgeville on the 21st instant, WILLIAM W. CARNES Esq. in the 39th year of his age.

Died at his residence in Carnesville, Georgia on Tuesday the 1st December inst. at 10 o'clock P.M. of the consumption of the lungs, Col. JAMES C. TERRELL, aged 29 years and 24 days, leaving a widowed mother and numerous friends... was the beloved representative, elected in 1834, of the northwestern section of the State; in his 24th year was the honored representative of his native county (Franklin) in the legislature of his native state. (long eulogy)

Died on Wednesday the 10th instant, after an illness of 34 days continuance of the inflammation of the lungs, at his residence in Talbot county, Georgia, JOHN TURNER COX, Esquire, aged 37 years; leaves wife and an orphan child.

Died on the 14th instant at the residence of her father (Daniel Malone Esq.) in Jones county, Georgia, MRS. MARTHA JAMERSON, consort of Mr. William Jamerson, of Stewart county, in the 19th year of her age; leaves husband and an infant daughter.

8 January 1836

Died in Milledgeville on the 31st of December 1835, in the 36th year of his age, ORANGE GREEN, a native of Brandon, in Vermont. He had been for the last ten years a resident of this place; had left a wife and a tender infant.

Died in Jefferson county on the 22d of December 1835 after an illness of three weeks, MRS. ELIZABETH WALKER, widow of William Walker, deceased, in the 65th year of her age; for the last thirty years a worthy member of the Methodist Episcopal Church.

15 January 1836

Died in Milledgeville on the 11th instant, of pulmonary consumption, MRS. LUCINDA HUNT, consort of Wilkins Hunt, Esq., in her 29th year.

29 January 1836

Died at his residence in Muscogee county, Ga. of an inflammation of the stomach, on the 11th day of December 1835, JOHN OQUIN, a revolutionary soldier, in the 82d year of his age; has left an aged widow and eight children.

Died on the 11th instant at the residence of her father, Thomas Swift, after a protracted illness of near twelve months, MRS. HARRIET T. FURLOW, wife of James W. Furlow of Monroe county, Ga., aged 18 years 1 month and 9 days.

12 February 1836
    Died at his residence in Talbot county on the 18th ult. SAMUEL WINFREY,
    of a chronic disease of the lungs, bowels and liver, which terminated
    in a dropsical complaint; in his 47th year; member of the Methodist
    Church for many years; a kind husband and tender parent.

26 February 1836
    Died at his residence in Baldwin county on the 13th instant, the
    Rev. CHARLES MALONE, in the 67th year of his age.

    Died at his residence in Twiggs county on the 3d instant, of disease
    of the lungs which terminated in fever, MARK FAULK, in the 57th year
    of his age; an acceptable member of the Methodist Church for the last
    seven years; left a wife and several children.

    Died in Macon on the 4th instant, Col. ARCHIBALD DARRAGH, aged about
    48 years, a native of Pennsylvania, but for many years a resident of
    this vicinity.

    Died in Macon on the 30th ult. in the 61st year of his age, MR.
    ZACHARIAH SIMS, an old inhabitant of that city, and an industrious and
    most ingenious mechanic.

18 March 1836
    Died in Macon on Saturday evening the 5th inst., MRS. ANNA RALSTON,
    consort of Mr. David Ralston, of that city, aged about 38 years.

    Death of a volunteer -- MR. BENJAMIN BARNES, a member of the Putnam
    Feucibles (captain Merriwether) and who marched with that corps to
    Florida, and was honorable discharged on account of severe sickness,
    died in this city yesterday on his way home... (Augusta Chronicle)

25 March 1836
    Died in M'Donough, Henry county on Wednesday evening the 2d instant,
    WILLIAM RAGLAND Esq., in the 71st year of his age. He was born in
    Northampton county, North Carolina, and removed to Chatham county, in
    that State, where he resided until the year 1814, when he removed to
    Jasper county, Georgia, and from thence to Henry. Towards the close of
    the Revolutionary war, although quite a youth, he was in the service of
    his country, and was taken prisoner, together with a number of others,
    by the Tories at colonel Alstons' house on Deep river; an acceptable
    member of the Methodist Episcopal Church.

21 April 1836
    The honorable JAMES POLHILL, Judge of the Southern Circuit, died at his
    residence in Hawkinsville on Saturday night last.

28 April 1836
    Died in Warrenton on Wednesday morning last in the 54th year of his
    age, DENNIS L. RYAN; elected to the legislature of the state; for many
    years a member of the Methodist Church... (Augusta Constitutionalist).

    Died in Milledgeville on Sunday evening last, MR. GEORGE W. KING, long
    a resident of this place.

5 May 1836

Died at Bainbridge, Decatur county, Georgia on the 25th ult.
MRS. ANN LESTER (consort of Mr. William C. Lester), in the 29th year
of her age, leaving seven small orphans to experience the irreparable
loss of a mother, and taking her newly born infant with her to moulder
by her side; member of the Baptist Church for six years.

19 May 1836

Died at her residence in Monroe county, Georgia on the morning of the
7th instant, MRS. ISABEL THOMAS, (consort of Mr. John H. Thomas) in
the 26th year of her age, leaving three helpless orphans to suffer an
irreparable loss; joined the Methodist Church at about age 23.

2 June 1836

Pained to announce the death of ANDERSON W. WILLIAMS, son of Colonel
Zachariah Williams, of Columbia county. He was slain by the hand of
the ruthless savage in defending the attack on the town of Roanoke, in
this State, on the morning of the 9th ultimo...received the fatal ball
in his forehead; was in the 21st year of his age and was engaged in
establishing a plantation on the Alabama shore of the Chattahoochee
river; leaves sisters, brothers and parents. (Augusta Constitutionalist,
27th ult.)

Died at Clifton in the county of Baldwin on the night of the 22d ultimo,
MRS. MARY BRYAN, wife of John S. Thomas Esq. after a short but painful
illness.

9 June 1836

Died at Clifton in the county of Baldwin on the night of the 22d ultimo,
MRS. MARY BRYAN THOMAS, wife of John S. Thomas Esq., after a short but
painful illness. Her own mother died when she was yet a child, and her
father Neyle Esq. having married again, sent Mrs. Thomas and her sister,
Miss Neyle, to the North, where they were educated, and remained until
their age and requirements fitted them for entering on the duties of
social and elegant life. Her grandmother was a daughter of Jonathan Bryan,
Esq., one of the first settlers of Georgia, and one of the firmest patriots
of the revolution, and was married to John Morel Esq. also attached to
the principles of the revolution, of which marriage Mrs. Thomas and her
surviving weeping sister, with others long since deceased, are the issue.
Leaves husband and four infant children; was a member of the Episcopal
Church.

23 June 1836

Died at his residence near Milledgeville on the 21st instant, AUGUSTIN
HARRIS Esq. in the fullness of his years. He was a man of a mild and
benevolent Christian spirit, and possessed in a high degree the esteem
and affection of this community.

30 June 1836

Died at the residence of J.L. Calhoun in Gerard, Alabama, on the night
of the 15th instant, of bilious fever, WILLIAM J. MORGAN, second son of
Stokely Morgan, late of Jasper county, Georgia, deceased, aged 16 years
5 months 28 days.

12 July 1836

Died in Milledgeville on the 2d instant, of pulmonary consumption, MR. CHARLES K. DANIEL, in the 19th year of his age; was a soldier in Captain Merriwether's company; and his fatal disease was contracted during the expedition to Florida.

Died on Wednesday the 25th of May last, MR. ANTHONY WINSTON WALKER, one of the Jefferson company of cavalry. He reached Louisville on Friday the 13th May from Florida, quite sick; was taken to the house of L.B. Bostick Esq...death swept him away, in the 27th year of his age.

2 August 1836

Died in Milledgeville on the 31st ultimo, of hemarhage of the lungs, MR. WILLIAM R. JACKSON, formerly of Virginia, but for several years past a resident of this place.

23 August 1836

Died on the 7th instant in Jones county, Ga. in the 24th year of her age, MRS. ELIZABETH M. COOK, consort of Jones E. Cook Esq.; leaves husband and three small children; an acceptable member of the Methodist Church.

Died on the 8th instant at his father's residence in Twiggs county, MR. HIRAM BEDINGFIELD, in the 25th year of his age; leaves parents.

30 August 1836

Died on Monday the 22d instant at 12 o'clock in Macon, the Rev. JOHN HOWARD, of the Methodist Episcopal Church, in the 45th year of his age. He was recovering from an attack of bilious fever...when an attack of cholera morbus supervened and in a few days terminated his existence. (with long eulogy)

Died in Suggsville, Alabama on the 7th instant, after an illness of five days, MR. THOMAS MOUNGER, printer. He had recently returned from Texas, where he had been engaged in the military service of that country.

Died at their residence near Eatonton on the 11th day of August, MRS. LAVINIA HOLT, wife of colonel Pulaski Holt, in the 32d year of her age.

6 September 1836

Died at Midway on the 16th ultimo in the 36th year of his age, MR. ALYAH STEELE, late steward of the Manual Labour Institute near Milledgeville. He was a man of high literary attainments.

Died at her father's residence in Jones county on Saturday evening the 27th ultimo, after a short but severe illness, MISS AMANDA BROWN, daughter of Mr. Robin Brown, in the 20th year of her age. (short eulogy)

27 September 1836

Died on Wednesday the 14th instant, in the ninth district of Houston county, Ga. JOHN G. BELL (youngest child of Archibald C. and Margaret M'Intyre), aged 2 years and 3 months.

Died suddenly on the 12th instant in Zebulon, Pike county, MISS NANCY ADAMS, daughter of the late General David Adams.

Died on the 10th instant at the house of William Morgan, near Greenville, Meriwether county, Georgia, a young man who said that his name was REUBEN BURRISS; he came to the house of Mr. Morgan on the last day of August last; he was travelling on foot without money, and almost in a state of nakedness; he was an entire stranger, and his mind appeared to be much impaired; he said that he came from Charleston, South Carolina, which place he left about seven months since, where his father still lived, whose name is John Burriss; he was laboring under some painful disease when he arrived, which the physicians considered typhus fever; after lingering some ten days he died. (Charleston papers to copy notice)

4 October 1836

Died at his residence in Jasper county, of cholera morbus, on Wednesday the 21st ult., MR. ANDREW WELDON, in the 69th year of his age; was a native Georgian and had lived 23 years in the county of Jasper; leaves a widow and several children.

11 October 1836

Died at his residence in Telfair county, General JOHN COFFEE, a representative from Georgia in the congress of the United States.

Died at Eatonton, CHARLES P. GORDON Esq., a virtuous man and a distinguished jurist.

18 October 1836

Died in Jasper county on Friday the 30th ult. MR. JOSEPH A. WILSON, aged 25 years; leaves a widow and four small children.

Died on the 2d instant in Talbot county, Georgia, in the 25th year of her age, MRS. JANE P. CLEMENTS, consort of Jacob A. Clements Esq. Was an acceptable member of the Methodist Church; leaves husband and four small children. (short eulogy)

Died in Milledgeville on Tuesday the 4th inst., after a painful and protracted illness of eighteen months, MR. ANDREW DUBOURG, in the 52d year of his age. Was a native of Bordeaux, France; had been a citizen of the United States during the last thirty years of his life, and a worthy and highly respected member of this community for the last eighteen.

Died in Houston county on the 1st inst. of congestive fever, captain JOHN MARCUS ALLEN.

Died in Athens on the 29th ult. Rev. SAMUEL B. PRESSLEY, professor of Moral Philosophy and Belles Lettres in the University of Georgia, after a severe illness of three weeks.

1 Nov 1836

Another revolutionary soldier gone! Died on the 2d ultimo after an illness of eleven days, at his residence in Columbia county, Ga., MR. ELIAS WELLBORN. Served his country as a soldier during the revolutionary struggle. He served in Gates' army when he was defeated at Camden, South Carolina, and was at the battle fought at Eutaw Springs in the same state; for several years was a member of the Baptist

Died suddenly on the 12th instant in Zebulon, Pike county, MISS
NANCY ADAMS, daughter of the late General David Adams.

Died on the 10th instant at the house of William Morgan, near
Greenville, Meriwether county, Georgia, a young man who said that
his name was REUBEN BURRISS; he came to the house of Mr. Morgan on
the last day of August last; he was travelling on foot without money,
and almost in a state of nakedness; he was an entire stranger, and
his mind appeared to be much impaired; he said that he came from
Charleston, South Carolina, which place he left about seven months
since, where his father still lived, whose name is John Burriss;
he was laboring under some painful disease when he arrived, which the
physicians considered typhus fever; after lingering some ten days he
died. (Charleston papers to copy notice)

4 October 1836
Died at his residence in Jasper county, of cholera morbus, on
Wednesday the 21st ult., MR. ANDREW WELDON, in the 69th year of his
age; was a native Georgian and had lived 23 years in the county of
Jasper; leaves a widow and several children.

11 October 1836
Died at his residence in Telfair county, General JOHN COFFEE, a
representative from Georgia in the congress of the United States.

Died at Eatonton, CHARLES P. GORDON Esq., a virtuous man and a
distinguished jurist.

18 October 1836
Died in Jasper county on Friday the 30th ult. MR. JOSEPH A. WILSON,
aged 25 years; leaves a widow and four small children.

Died on the 2d instant in Talbot county, Georgia, in the 25th year
of her age, MRS. JANE P. CLEMENTS, consort of Jacob A. Clements Esq.
Was an acceptable member of the Methodist Church; leaves husband and
four small children. (short eulogy)

Died in Milledgeville on Tuesday the 4th inst., after a painful and
protracted illness of eighteen months, MR. ANDREW DUBOURG, in the
52d year of his age. Was a native of Bordeaux, France; had been a
citizen of the United States during the last thirty years of his life,
and a worthy and highly respected member of this community for the
last eighteen.

Died in Houston county on the 1st inst. of congestive fever, captain
JOHN MARCUS ALLEN.

Died in Athens on the 29th ult. Rev. SAMUEL B. PRESSLEY, professor of
Moral Philosophy and Belles Lettres in the University of Georgia, after
a severe illness of three weeks.

1 Nov 1836
Another revolutionary soldier gone! Died on the 2d ultimo after an
illness of eleven days, at his residence in Columbia county, Ga.,
MR. ELIAS WELLBORN. Served his country as a soldier during the
revolutionary struggle. He served in Gates' army when he was defeated
at Camden, South Carolina, and was at the battle fought at Eutaw
Springs in the same state; for several years was a member of the Baptist

31 January 1837

Another soul has fled. Notice of the death of MR. MARK FAULK, son of Mrs. Milbry Faulk and Mr. Mark Faulk of Twiggs County, He died at his home, the place of his nativity, in Twiggs County, at eight o'clock in the morning, 1st January 1837, in the 22nd year of his age, of a disease of the stomach and bowels... (long eulogy)

7 February 1837

Died in Milledgeville on the 27th ultimo, MISS ANN ELIZA SMITH, in the 17th year of her age...early death was caused by a dreadful burn...her protracted sufferings terminated in death on the 19th day after the accident.

Died in Talbot county on the 8th ultimo, MR. EPHRAIM MABRY, Esq., of Cedar Valley, Paulding County, Georgia. Was a man much esteemed by his neighbors and acquaintances. Has left a wife and four children.

14 February 1837

Died at his residence in Monroe County on the 4th instant, JOHN SHOCKLEY, Esq., in the 51st year of his age. He was violently attacked with pleurisy, which terminated his earthly career in seven or eight days; for sixteen years a worthy and acceptable member of the Baptist Church; leaves a disconsolate family (long eulogy).

Died in Milledgeville on the 7th instant, ADAM WILKINSON, aged 56 years, formerly of Charles City County, Virginia but for the last 26 years a resident of this place.

21 February 1837

Died on the 31st of January last, JOSEPH S. NEELY, of Thomas County. He had a severe attack of measles, followed by an inflammatory fever, which seemed to resist the power of medicine and physicians. Was confined twenty-four days and suffered indescribable pain; has left a wife and one child.

14 March 1837

Died in Sparta on the 11th instant, DAVID E. BUTTS, Esquire, after an illness of seven days. His disease was Bilious Pleurisy.

Distressing accident. MR. A. HARDIS of Beech Island was returning home from a visit to his sister, on Tuesday evening last, when his horse took fright, became unmanageable, and dashed him against a tree with a momentum which immediately terminated his existence. Was 35 years old and has left a wife and one child. (Augusta Courier, 7th instant).

21 March 1837

Died in Milledgeville on the 17th instant, Major THOMAS H. KENAN, late United States Marshal for the district of Georgia, aged 63 years. He was a native of North Carolina, and had been for more than thirty years a citizen of Milledgeville.

Died in Milledgeville on the morning of the 14th inst. MRS. MARGARET S. WRIGHT, consort of Mr. Pryor Wright, of this place, in the 35th year of her age; member of Methodist Episcopal Church; leaves husband and children (long eulogy).

28 March 1837
Horrid outrage! MR. JOHN GREGORY, a citizen of this place, was found
on Monday morning last, near the corner of Troup and Crawford sts.
badly beaten and nearly lifeless. He died on the following day. The
author of the barbarous deed is unknown, but we are informed that
suspicion rests on a free boy of color, by the name of Nelson. The
deceased left a wife and one promising child. (Columbus Enquirer, 16th inst).

4 April 1837
Died in Milledgeville on the 28th ult., MR. WALTER JONES (Printer),
a native of Virginia but a citizen of this place for about thirty years.

18 April 1837
Died in Milledgeville on the 12th day of April, MRS. ELIZABETH A. FOARD,
consort of Mr. Thomas Foard, in the 52d year of her age; a member of the
Methodist Episcopal Church for 31 years; leaves husband, children and orphan.
(with eulogy).

Died in Harris County on the 3d inst. of congestive fever in the 29th year
of her age, MRS. ELIZABETH BLAKE HOLSEY, consort of Hon. Hopkins Holsey.
(long article giving details surrounding the death)

25 April 1837
Died in Hawkinsville on the 18th instant, DELAMAR CLAYTON, Esq. A victim
of despair from repeated domestic afflictions, this estimable man fell in
the prime of life by his own hand.

Died in Milledgeville on the 22d inst. GENERAL D.B. MITCHELL. An emigrant
from Scotland in his early youth, he has been a conspicuous man in Georgia,
has filled many honorable stations, and twice filled the Executive Chair.

Departed this life at the residence of her mother in this county on the
morning of the 20th inst., MRS. ARAMINTA D. MOORE, aged 18 years 8 months
and 20 days; for several years an exemplary member of the Methodist Church;

Died on Saturday the 15th inst. in Baldwin county, MRS. JANE M. TORRANCE,
in the 34th year of her age, the wife of William H. Torrance, Esq. and
daughter of the late Peter Crawford, of Columbia county. Was member of the
Methodist Church.

(From the Macon Messenger) - Died on the 15th inst. in the 60th year of his
age, Major SOLOMON GROCE, an old and highly respectable citizen of Bibb County.
(short eulogy)

2 May 1837
Died of Erysipelas in this city on the 17th inst. MR. ROBERT PATTON, in the
49th year of his age. He was a native of North Carolina, where he learned the
watch-making business, but has worked generally at the Mill-wright business since his
coming to this state, which was about 17 or 18 years ago. He was a first rate
mechanic and an honest man.

Died at his residence in Baldwin county on the 10th day of April, MR. WILLIAM WILD,
in the 35th year of his age. Has left a widow and two small children.
(short eulogy)

Fatal accident. MR. E. THATCHER of Burke County was last week engaged in
repairing the lock of his gun when it accidentally went off and its whole contents
lodged in the body of his wife who instantly dropped dead, at his feet!

May 30, 1837
    Died at his residence in Clinton, Jones county, on Monday morning the
    14th inst. SAMUEL LOWTHER, Esq. in the 49th year of his age.

13 June 1837
    Died in Columbus on Friday evening the 2d instant, MR. THOMAS W. HOWE,
    formerly of the city of Boston, but for the last two months a resident
    of this place...An unfortunate difficulty took place between himself
    and a young man by the name of Richard C. Ridgway, who sought a meeting --
    few words passed between them, when Ridgway drew a pistol and shot him
    down. The ball entering on the left side of the neck and ranging
    downwards into the right breast. The unhappy victim survived until the
    next evening, when death put an end to his sufferings. His remains
    were conveyed to the Methodist Church, where a funeral ceremony was
    performed by the Rev. Dr. Pierce - and followed to the grave by a large
    number of friends and citizens. Ridgway is now confined to our Jail,
    to await his trial at the next term of our Superior Court, in October
    next. (Columbus Sentinel, 8th inst.)

    Died in Milledgeville, Georgia on the 25th of April last, of Consumption,
    MISS MARY ANN HERTY, aged 28 years.

    Died in the city of Macon, at Major Peter J. Williams' on the 31st ult.
    MISS MARGARET VEITCH, a native of Maryland. Miss Veitch had resided
    in Milledgeville nine years, chiefly as a Tutress, was an acceptable
    member of the Presbyterian Church. (Telegraph)

20 June 1837
    Died on the 18th instant, aged 23 years 11 months and 21 days,
    MRS. ELIZABETH J. KEY, wife of Rev. C. W. Key, pastor of the Methodist
    Episcopal Church in Milledgeville, and daughter of Rev. and Mrs. Joshua
    and Ann Hames of Jasper county; member of the church nearly eleven years;
    (short eulogy)

27 June 1837
    Died at his residence in Baldwin county, BENJAMIN GOODWIN AYERS, in
    his 48th year. He walked to church on the Sabbath day, near three miles
    and back and was a corpse on Thursday following, showing to us the
    uncertainty of life... has left a widow and relations to mourn his
    departure.

18 July 1837
    Died at his residence in Putnam county on the 30th of June, WILLIAM A.
    SLAUGHTER, Esq. in the 45th year of his age...member of the Methodist
    Episcopal Church for more than 22 years (with short eulogy).

25 July 1837
    Died in Jones county on the 15th instant of bilious fever, MRS. LOUISA M. HUNT,
    consort of Alexander J. Hunt, Esq. in the 26th year of her age. (short eulogy)

    Died on the 20th of July in the 53d year of her age, MRS. ELIZA RUTHERFORD,
    the wife of Wms. Rutherford. (with short eulogy).

    Another murder. Regret to announce the murder of CAPT. L. GILLELAND of
    Alachua a few days since. His horse was found dead on the road from Suwannee
    to Newnansville with his hat and blanket laying beside the horse...his body
    was found at Itchotnchny springs.

8 August 1837

Died in this place on the 31st ultimo of Cholera Infantum, MARY OPHELIA, infant daughter of Alfred M. and Sarah S. NISBET, aged 16 months and 3 weeks.

15 August 1837

Died at the Helicon Spring on the morning of the 1st instant, of protracted liver complaint, MRS. MARGARET, consort of James L. DeLAUNVY, of Milledgeville.

22 August 1837

Died at his residence in Meriwether county, Ga. on the 10th of August 1837, the Rev. HOBSON MORGAN, in the 43rd year of his age...member of the Methodist Episcopal Church nearly 27 years; leaves wife and children. (with long eulogy).

Died in Milledgeville on the 10th instant, CATHARINE JOHNSTON, youngest daughter of Mr. and Mrs. HERTY, aged 7 months and 12 days.

29 August 1837

Died of inflammation of the brain at his residence in Jasper county on the 6th instant, MR. EDWIN S. SCISSON.

5 September 1837

Died at his residence in Elbert county on the 30th ult. GEORGE COOK, Esq. He was with an exception of two the oldest lawyer in the State of Georgia. He was born on the 18th of November 1764; when young, he took a part in the revolution. His mind was of the first order though uneducated...

26 September 1837

Tribute of Respect by the students of Midway Seminary to their fellow student THOMAS J. GORDON... tribute dated 22d inst.

Died in Monticello, Jasper county, on the 26th of August last, MR. EDWARD HICKS, in the 37th year of his age. Was a native of Providence, Rhode Island, but for the last eighteen years a resident of Monticello; has left a wife and numerous friends to mourn his death.

3 October 1837

(From the Washington, Ga. Spy)-- Following melancholy intelligence contained in the Wheeling (Va.) Times reached us last week...Died in this city, on Sunday evening, September 3rd, at the residence of his brother-in-law, George A. Clark, Esq., COL. WILLIAM C. LYMAN, of Watkinsville, Georgia, in the 45th year of his age.

Died in the city of Columbus on the 25th ult. MRS. ELIZABETH S. McKEEN, consort of Thomas C. McKeen, Esq. (formerly Miss Elizabeth Robinson of this place) in the 20th year of her age, after an illness of nine hours.

Died in Milledgeville on Wednesday 20th ult. at the house of Mrs. Rutherford, MR. THOS. J. GORDON, eldest son of Gen. Gordon, of Jones county, in the 17th year of his age; member of Midway Seminary.

7 November 1837

Died in Monroe, Walton county, on the 21st day of October 1837, MRS. MILCAH STROUD, daughter of Thomas Trammell, late of Upson county dec'd, and wife of Orion Stroud, Esq., in the 37th year of her age...leaves husband

and eight children, the youngest of whom was not quite three months
old; native of the county of Clark, and was for 13 years an orderly
member of the Methodist Episcopal Church (with long eulogy).

14 November 1837
    Death of a Revolutionary hero. CAPT. RICHARD BOHUN BAKER, the last of
    the survivors of the band of Heroes engaged during the Rev. War in the
    defence of Fort Moultrie, died on Monday night at that post, the scene
    of his gallant conduct, aged 80 years and 2 months.

21 November 1837
    Died in this city on the 11th instant after a short illness, DR. HARRIS
    LOOMIS, aged 37 years. He removed from Fayetteville, North Carolina to
    this city about two years since...a man of considerable acquirements
    as a Botanist, and had done much in collecting and examining the vegetable
    productions incident to Carolina and Georgia. (Macon Messenger, 16th inst.)

28 November 1837
    Died at his residence in this county on the 23d instant, of a disease
    with which he had been afflicted for the last 16 years of his life,
    MR. JAMES D. JARRATT, in the 31st year of his life.

19 December 1837
    Shocking accident. MR. JOHN TERRY, of this county, passed through this
    place on Wednesday last, with a load of cotton, on his way to Augusta,
    and when a few miles from here, in going down a steep hill, his team
    became unmanageable, and by some means he was thrown down, and the wagon
    wheels passed directly over his head and other parts of his body, producing
    instant death. Lawrenceville, Gwinnett Co., Ga. November 27, 1837.
    (Athens Banner)

26 December 1837
    Died at his residence in Twiggs county on Saturday 2d inst., ROBERT F. GLENN,
    aged within one month of 25 years. (with short eulogy).

23 January 1838
    Died at Pontotoc, Mississippi on the 5th instant, DR. ALEXANDER S. TENNILLE,
    a native of Washington county, Georgia, aged 26 years...left brother,
    mother and other relations (with long eulogy).

30 January 1838
    Died at his residence in Henry county, Georgia on the 12th inst.,
    WILLIS MOORE, Esq., in the 36th year of his age...bilious pleurisy, after
    an illness of two weeks, terminated his stay on earth; left wife and
    family (with long eulogy).

6 February 1838
    Horrid murder. We learn from a correspondent in the upper part of
    Spartanburg District that THOMAS SMITH was murdered in that neighborhood
    on the 16th inst. by Asa Bone...

13 February 1838

(From the Missouri Saturday News). Died at the residence of Major J.B. Brant in this city (St. Louis) on the 3d ult., MRS. ANN BENTON, aged near 80 years. Was the mother of Colonel T.H. Benton of the United States Senate. (short eulogy).

6 March 1838

Died in this place on the 3d instant, MR. HILMAN B. HUTCHINS, printer, a native of Charleston, S.C., but for the last four years a resident of Milledgeville.

27 March 1838

Died on the 10th inst. at his residence in Monticello, Ga. DR. MOSES CHAMPION, aged 46. Was a native of Massachusetts, but for many years past resided in Monticello, and had been engaged in a very extensive practice.

Died on the 18th inst. at his residence in Monticello, Ga. DR. JAMES B. LEWIS, after a short illness; member of the Baptist Church; had been engaged for several years in the practice of medicine in Jasper county; left a wife and three children.

Died at Lowndesboro, Lowndes county (Ala) on the 21st ult., MRS. MARY B. HARRISON, wife of Mr. Thomas Harrison, in the 24th year of her age.

10 April 1838

Died at the residence of his father in Hancock county on the 20th of March last, JEREMIAH S. SANFORD, in the 21st year of his age; had paid a visit to his friends in Putnam county but a few days before his death, and appeared to be in good health; (long eulogy)

Departed this life in Covington, Georgia on Monday the 19th of March, MARY ANN FOSTER, consort of Dr. C.E.F.W. Campbell, and daughter of Abner and Jane G. Pinder, of Oglethorpe, Georgia; leaves husband and infant.

17 April 1838

Died in this city on the morning of the 12th instant at 8 o'clock, MR. WILLIAM A. GODWIN, in the 19th year of his age. The deceased has for several years assisted his widowed mother in superintending the house of entertainment kept by her in this place, where the disorder became seated which terminated his life. He was afflicted for several months with Pulmonary Consumption. (short eulogy)

24 April 1838

Died on Sunday the 16th instant at five o'clock P.M., STEVENS THOMAS, Esq. one of the oldest and most respected citizens of this place. He was among the earliest settlers of Athens. (Southern Banner - Athens).

1 May 1838

Died in the city of Savannah on the 25th of March last of dropsy of
the chest, MR. JOHN RAIFORD SCARBOROUGH, son of Miles Scarborough, Esq.
of Meriwether county, in the 27th year of his age. Had been for fourteen
years a member of the Methodist Church.

22 May 1838

THOMAS BRADFORD, Esq., successor to Dr. Franklin, and the oldest Printer
and Editor in the Union, died on the 7th inst. at Philadelphia, in the
94th year of his age.

Another Revolutionary patriot gone. Major JAMES ROBINSON, better known as
"Horse Shoe Robinson", died at his residence in Tuscaloosa county, Alabama,
on the 8th April 1838 in the 79th year of his age.

Another Rev. patriot has been translated to another world...
Col. JOHN SHELLMAN...served two campaigns in the MD. line at the commencement
of the war; was at the battle of White Plains; and subsequently a captain
of the volunteer corps of cavalry from Maryland, raised in part for the
protection of the state of Virginia. His mortal remains were yesterday
attended to the grave...military honors awarded him by the volunteer corps
of the 1st Reg. under command of Major Wylly. (Sav. Georgian, 14th inst.)

12 June 1838

The body of Colonel FOWLER, of the US Army, was found near Madison on
Sunday the 13th inst. His Commission, a gold watch and $500 in treasury notes,
were found upon his person. (Cincinnati Daily News).

Died in this city, of consumption, on Sunday morning last, CHARLES L. BRADLEY,
in the 37th year of his age. Was a native of New Haven, Conn. but for the
last eleven years a resident of this state - five of which he has spent in
this community.

Died at his residence in Jones county in the 71st year of his age,
WILLIAM JOHNSON, Senr...spent his early years and was educated among the
Friends or Quakers... (with eulogy)

19 June 1838

Died at his residence in Gwinnett county, Geo. on the morning of the 10th inst.
after a short but painful illness of billious or cramp cholic, MR. ROBERT
CAMPBELL, in the 37th year of his age...leaves an aged father and mother,
widow and four children; an acceptable member of the Presbyterian Church.
(with short eulogy)

3 July 1838

Died on Wednesday evening 27th ult. at the residence of Col. Thomas Haynes
in this city, MR. JESSE RICH, after a long and painful illness.

Died at his residence in this city on Friday morning last, after a few days
illness, MR. GEORGE ROOT, a highly respected merchant and citizen of this
city for a number of years past.

Died in this city on Saturday evening last, MRS. MARY ROSE, wife of
William Rose, in the 28th year of her age; a native of North Carolina but
a resident of this state for the last two years.

10 July 1838

Died near his residence in Putnam county on the 26th June,
MR. ELISHA MATHIS, aged 66 years; member of the Baptist church.
(with long eulogy)

Murder. We learn that a MR. DUNN, residing near Lexington in
Oglethorpe county, was murdered on Sunday last while on his way from
Church, and within a short distance of his home. He was found stabbed
in several places and his throat horribly cut - indeed, his head was
nearly severed from his body. (Athens Banner, 30th ult.)

17 July 1838

Died in Macon on the 5th inst., WILLIS T. SAGE (Printer), aged about
39 years; native of Greenfield, Mass. but had resided in Macon for the
last eleven years; was buried with military honors by the Bibb Cavalry, of
which corps he was a member.

Died on the 29th of June of palsy, at the residence of Stephen Hoge Esq.
in Decatur county, MISS SARAH GARDNER, in the 67th year of her age; had
lived in the family of Mr. Hoge for the last thirty years - for the last
two years has been severely afflicted with palsy and accute rheumatism.

Died at the residence of his father in Talbot county on the 10th inst.
while on a visit for the benefit of her health, Mrs. SOPHIA BOATRIGHT,
consort of Rolla Boatright, of Washington county, in the 34th year of her
age, leaving a disconsolate husband and two children; a pious member of
the Methodist church.

24 July 1838

Died near Clinton, Jones county, on the 19th of June, MRS. MARTHA W.,
consort of Mr. Thomas H. BRAY, aged 27 years, leaving two small children;
a professor of religion for upwards of seven years and an acceptable member
of the Methodist Episcopal Church... (with long eulogy)

Fatal casualty. On Tuesday evening of last week, a catastrophe occurred
near Midway, about a mile from M'ville, which terminated in the death of
MR. JAMES GORDON, a native of Scotland, but lately a resident of Sandersville,
Washington county. Mr. Gordon was on a return visit to this place, upon a
fractious and unruly horse, when he was thrown to the ground with such violence
as to fracture his skull...

Death of an old patriot. The last soldier of the old French War in Canada
is gone. Died in Warren county, Tennessee on the 8th of June, MR. JOHN LUSK
(pronounced LISK, in his native Dutch) at the advanced age of 104 years. He
was born on Staten Island, NY 5 Nov 1734 and was of Dutch extraction. Was in
regular service for well nigh sixty years. He commenced his career in the
Army in the war Acadie commonly called the French war, when about 20 years of
age, and served through the whole of it. Was a soldier at the siege of Quebec,
fought in the memorable action of the Plains of Abraham 79 years ago, saw the
brave Gen. Wolfe fall...was also at the conquest of Acadie, now called
Newfoundland, by Generals Amherst and Shirley, and assisted in the dispersion
of the captured French through the colonies of New England, by the Anglo-Americans.

More victims to the savage barbarity. By the arrival of a gentleman from Garey's Ferry on the 4th inst. we have received intelligence of the murder of a whole family named GWINN, who resided on the Sante Fe river. They fell victims to savage barbarity; a father, mother and two children were found murdered at their residence on the 2d inst.; a daughter about 13 years of age is missing... (St. Augustine Herald, 7th inst.)

31 July 1838

We learn by the Lexington, Ky. Intelligencer of the 17th inst. that PETER W. GRAYSON, Esq., of Texas, committed suicide at Bean's Station a few days before by shooting himself with a pistol through the head. Mr. G. was on his way from Texas to Washington city, having received and accepted from the Govt. of Texas the appointment of Minister Plenipotentiary to the Govt. of the US. Mr. G. was a native of Kentucky.

MR. JOSEPH STEVENSON of Madison county, Ky. committed suicide on the 1st inst. by shooting himself through the head with a rifle.

MRS. ELIZABETH ALVERSON, of Gurraud county, Ky. was found dead in the barn of her husband, Mr. John G. Alverson, on the 3d inst. having hung herself with a rope attached to one of the joists.

7 Aug 1838

Melancholy and fatal accident. Yesterday morning about seven o'clock an industrious and respectable mechanic named WARREN MITCHELL, while working at the new Patent Office Building, was suddenly hurried into eternity under the following circumstances. The unfortunate man was sitting upon a huge block of stone as it was being hoisted from the floor of the building to its intended position. Unfortunately the rope suddenly gave way, when the stone struck the column below, broke in two, and wedged the poor man between part of it and the column. (Nat. Intelligencer).

14 Aug 1838

The negro man GEORGE, the property of P. STOVALL, Esq., who was sentenced to be hung for the crime of Rape, was executed yesterday at a few minutes after 11 o'clock. He confessed his guilt before he reached the scaffold. (Constitutionalist, 10th inst.)

21 Aug 1838

Tallahassee, August 4. The following letter from Col. James Gadsden gives an account of another horrid murder committed by savages, near Bailey's Mill, a few miles from Col. G's, entirely within the frontier border...Wed. morning 1 Aug 1838 - the early part of last evening MR. SINGLETARY, his wife and two children were shockingly murdered in this neighborhood. But one of the family, a girl of about 5 years of age, miraculously escaped to tell the melancholy tidings of her parents and sisters.

The Natchez Free Trader of the 9th inst. states that Messrs. DRANE and DINKINS, citizens of Canton, Madison county, Miss., both gentlemen of high respectability, fought a few days ago near that place, with double barreled shot guns, and were both killed.

28 Aug 1838

Died at Mobile on the 17th inst. after a short illness,
MRS. ANN MATILDA HEARD.

11 Sep 1838

Another Rev. patriot gone. Died at his residence in Greene county,
Georgia on the morning of the 29th ult., Major OLIVER PORTER, in the
75th year of his age...after the revolution he emigrated to this state
from Prince Edward county, Virginia, and was among the first settlers of
the county of Greene, where his patriotic services were again put in requisition
in suppressing the ravages of a savage Indian enemy; was a member of the
representative branch of the State legislature; was also on one occasion a
State Elector of President and Vice President of the U. States...has left a
large family connection; for past 25 years an acceptable member of the
Baptist Church.

18 Sep 1838

Proclamation by Gov. George Gilmer offering a $200 reward for the
apprehension of William Slay for the murder of his wife WLIZABETH SLAY
on 1st September instant, in DeKalb county.

2 Oct 1838

From Texas. New Orleans, Sept. 13. MR. W.D. DURHAM, a native of Norfolk
county, England, died at Houston on the 26th August, aged 24 years.

9 Oct 1838

The Nahville Whig of the 11th ult. says that Pleasant Watson of DeKalb county
and a MR. CARMICHAEL of Alabama were the principles in an affray at
Livingston, Overton County, last week, which terminated in the death of the
latter...the dispute grew out of a horse race.

16 Oct 1838

A difficulty occurred on Tuesday evening last in this city between
MR. E. PLANT and a man by the name of JOHN BRADY, which resulted in the
death of the latter. A Coroner's Inquest was held and a verdict given that
the deed was committed in self-defense. (Macon Telegraph, 9th inst.)

On Saturday evening last an affray took place between GEORGE S. LOVING and
WILLIAM W. THOMPSON, which also terminated in the death of the latter. We
understand that Loving made his escape. (Macon Telegraph, 9th inst.)

Shocking murder. We have a letter from a gentleman at North Bennington (Vt.)
dated Wed. morning, stating that on Tuesday evening the wife of PHILEMON BATES,
of that place, was shot through the head by her husband's brother, Archibald,
with a rifle...At the moment of this fiendlike murder, Mrs. Bates was sitting
with her infant in her arms... (N.Y. Commercial Adv.)

Murder. A young man named THOMAS HAMILTON was stabbed on the night of the
24th Sept. at Spring Hill (Ala.). The deceased had been drinking and was
returning home, when he met his grandfather, who was also inebriated. An
altercation ensued and the latter struck the young man and stabbed him in
the belly, of which wound he died in nine or ten hours afterwards. The
murderer's name is Benjamin Alexander - he is 90 years of age.

Died at Athens on the evning of the 2d inst. after a short but violent
illness, WILLIAM R. DAWSON, eldest son of the Hon. William C. Dawson, in
the 19th year of his age.

Died at Athens on the 4th inst. MR. NATHAN ATKINSON, of Camden county, .
and a member of the senior class of Franklin College.

Died on Wed. the 12th inst. at the residence of his son, Mr. Jordan Ryals,
HENRY RYALS, at the advanced age of 110 years. He retained his faculties
to the last. He was one of the patriotic band who fought for the liberties
we enjoy.

Died in Washington on the 23d ult. MRS. EMILY A. POPE, consort of
Dr. John H. Pope, in the 39th year of her age.

23 Oct 1838
Proclamation by Gov. George R. Gilmer offering $200 reward for the
apprehension of Daniel V. Palmer for the murder of JAMES GUNN in Jasper
county 21 Aug 1838.

30 Oct 1838
Death of a Naval Officer. Comm. CREIGHTON, of the US Navy, died on
Saturday morning at the residence of his brother, near Sing Sing, New York.

A murder of the most revolting nature was committed upon the bodies of
MR. WILLIAM BAXTER and two of his children, a son and a daughter, on the
1st inst. near Pendleton, SC by a negro man...

Died in this city on the 24th inst. MR. P.A. KING, of Augusta, Ga., aged
23 years. He was a son of Dr. Wm. King of Green Co., Ga., and son-in-law
of Mr. Joseph Stovall, of this city...an affectionate husband and an esteemed
member of the Methodist Episcopal Church; leaves a young and bereaved widow.

Proclamation by Gov. George R. Gilmer offering a $200 reward for the
apprehension of George S. Loving for the murder of WILLIAM W. THOMPSON on
the 6th day of October in Bibb county.

6 Nov 1838
Died at the residence of his father in Baker county on the 18th ult.,
JACOB LUCAS, son of Mary C. and Thos. J. HOLMES, aged 3 years 4 months.

Died in Charleston, SC on Saturday the 27th ult. of the prevailing epidemic,
DR. D.F. NARDIN (editor of the Southern Botanic Journal), a native of France,
but for many years a resident of this country, aged 33 years...
(with short eulogy) (Charleston Courier)

13 Nov 1838
A Coroner's Inquest was held yesterday morning on the body of MRS. NANCY TINLEY
wife of William Tinley, of this county...came to her death by blows and
severe treatment received from her husband. (Chronicle & Sentinel, 10th inst.)

Died in this city on the evening of the 31st ultimo after a violent attack
of fever,Major OBADIAH ECHOLS, in the 31st year of his age. Was buried on
the evening of the 1st inst. with military honors by the Metripolitan Greys,
of which newly organized and spirited company he was an officer.

20 Nov 1838

Proclamation by Gov. George R. Gilmer offering $200 reward for the apprehension of John H. Hendricks for the murder of THOMAS R. MITCHELL on 22 Oct in Jasper county.

27 Nov 1838

Supposed murder. On the 13th inst. the body of a man was discovered in a hollow log, near Johnson's Mills in Jones county; apparently having been in that situation eight or ten days. On the body were sixteen or seventeen cuts and stabs; showing conclusively that he must have come to his death by foul means. Some papers were found on him, by which it appeared that his name was ELIAS M. ISAACS - some of them for purchase of Jewelry in Albany, Utica, and Syracuse, New York...while here the murdered man was engaged in peddling Jewelry, and claimed to have the value of three to four thousand dollars in watches, jewelry and money; which probably was the immediate cause of his murder... (Macon Messenger, 22d inst.)

4 Dec 1838

On Saturday the 27th ult. Wm. L. Yancy, Esq., who had been indicted for the murder of DR. EARLE, and convicted of manslaughter by the Jury at the Greenville Sessions, was sentenced by Judge Evans to an imprisonment of one year and a fine of $1500... (Charleston Mercury)

11 Dec 1838

Stop the murderers! $1000 reward will be paid by the undersigned for the apprehension of John Step and Solomon Step, who murdered MARTIN FRALEY, SEN. on the 8th Oct. inst., near Wolf's Ferry in Hardin county, Tennessee... the Steps formerly resided in Cherokee county, Georgia, and it is thought they will either make their way back to Georgia or strike for Texas. Signed: Sally Fraley, Henderson G. Fraley, Jackson Fraley, Samuel Fraley - and dated 20 Oct 1838.

Fatal rencontre. Affray took place on Monday the 3d inst. in Brunswick, Glynn county, Georgia, between JOHN A. WYLLY, Esq. and THOMAS F. HAZARD, Esq., both of St. Simon's Island, McIntosh county, in which the former gentleman was shot dead.

More Indian murders in Georgia. On Friday last, Nov. 23rd four men from Lowndes county were passing to Tradershill and were attacked at Mr. Isham Stephen's place by a party of Indians...young man named HURST and his horse were killed on the spot; MR. BOYD HILL mortally wounded.

18 Dec 1838

An affray occurred in Columbia, Tenn. on the 3d inst. between R.H. HAYES, Esq., Attorney at Law, and MR. WM. POLK, brother of the Hon. Jas. K. Polk. The parties met armed with pistols, exchanged shots, and Mr. Hayes was killed by a shot piercing his brain. The difficulty arose out of a jest.

25 Dec 1838

Proclamation by Gov. George R. Gilmer (of the state of Georgia) offering $200 reward for the apprehension of William Garrard who committed murder upon the body of HILLIARD J. BARKEDALE on 4th December inst. in Putnam county.

1 Jan 1839

Murder. A letter to the editors of the Macon Telegraph, from Pond Town, Geo., states that a wilful murder was committed in that village on the night of the 12th inst. on the body of a traveller named CHARLES B. HARDEN, a citizen of

Paulding County. Was about 45 years of age, one eye out; had wife and six
children...was murdered by a man of the name of Jacob Carter, of Marion County,
without any provocation. The murderer has been apprehended and lodged in jail.

8 Jan 1839

Fatal rencontre. On Friday last the 28th ult. a fatal rencontre took place
in the town of Washington, Autauga county, between JOHN TITTLE and
THOMAS J. TARLTON, which resulted in the death of the former...homicide
ruled justifiable. (Montgomery, Ala. Advertiser)

A homicide was committed in East Macon on Thursday last by a mechanic named
JOHN CHAPMAN on the body of his wife, by cutting her throat! (Macon Telegraph)

15 Jan 1839

Frozen to death. A gentleman writing from Dixon's Ferry, Arkansas, under
date of Nov. 26, relates account of the death of MR. STEPHEN CROOK, of
Prophetstown.

22 Jan 1839

Died at his residence in Alabama, four miles from Columbus, on Saturday
12th Jan., WILLIAM REDD, Esq., formerly of Greene county, Georgia, in the
64th year of his age.

5 Feb 1839

Death of GEN. BULL of Abbeville. From the Greenville, SC Mountaineer. Was
murdered on the night of the 27th ult. near his own dwelling...

12 Feb 1839

We learn that a murder was committed in the county of Crawford on the
26th ult. on the body of MILTON GLOVER, by Lewis Johnson, who has made
his escape.

Died on Thursday afternoon the 31st ultimo, MRS. JEAN MONCURE ORME, wife
of Richard M. Orme, one of the editors of the Southern Recorder...her chief
solitude seemed to her her infant only ten days old... (Recorder - long eulogy)

Died in Cassville on Wed. evening the 30th January 1839, Col. ZACHARIAH B.
HARGROVE, in the 39th year of his age. Leaves wife and five small children.

19 Feb 1839

The St. Josephs (Fla.) Times of the 3d inst. contains "puff" for the
"Magician and Ventriloquist" who is implicated in the murder of ISAACS, the
Jew peddler, in Jones county, for whose apprehension a reward of $300 is
offered by the Governor...

26 Feb 1839

JAMES TEMPLETON, convicted of   murder at the last term of the Superior
Court of Lumpkin county, has been sentenced to be hung on Friday the 5th of
April next.

The murderers of ISAACS. Col. Daniel M. Smith, Sheriff of Jones county,
left this city last evening with a requisition from Gov. Gilmer, on the
Executive of South Carolina, for the delivery of Henry Jones who, by his own
confession, was cognizant of the recent brutal murder in that county...

Sudden death. On Tuesday evening last I.T. Cushing, Coroner, was called to view the body of a man found dead in an out-house on the premises of the Globe Hotel. On the inquest, the deceased was recognized as MR. C.S. BRYAN, a respectable citizen of Twiggs county. It appeared he had recently arrived from Augusta, where he had been on the transaction of business, and had taken and paid for a seat home, in the stage that left on the evening of his decease; but on its departure he could not be found. It was supposed his death was occasioned by a fit. His remains were taken to Twiggs county for interment.

Accident. T.R. THOMPSON, Esq., a highly respectable young gentleman of Tuskaloosa, was recently, while hunting, killed by the accidental discharge of his gun. (Montgomery Advertiser, 22d inst.)

Atrocious murder. Letter dated Greenville, Butler county, Alabama, Feby 6th, states that on the evening of the 4th a most cruel murder was committed by one John Rabun upon the body of PETER MARTIN of that county, an aged and inoffensive man... (New Orleans Bee)

JOHN CHAPMAN, the murderer of his wife, is to be hung in Bibb county on Friday 22d of March next.

Died in Jones county on the 23d inst. MR. ISHAM CHOAT, in the 35th year of his age.

Proclamation by Gov. George R. Gilmer offering $200 reward for the apprehension of J.W. Coates and John Dickerson for murder committed in Jones county upon the body of a man named ELIAS or ICHABOD M. ISAACS.

5 Mar 1839

The execution of ARCHIBALD L. BATES for the murder of his brother's wife, MRS. HARRIET BATES, took place at Bennington, Vt. on the 8th inst....

Died at the house of Mrs. Catchings, of Jones county, on the 25th ult., MRS. FRANCES BONNER, relict of Capt. Richard Bonner, deceased, of Hancock county, aged about 80 years.

Died at his residence in Jasper county on the 7th inst. after a short illness of six days, SAMUEL BARBER, SENR., in the 66th year of his age; was among the early settlers of Jasper.

Another Rev. soldier gone! Died on Sunday the 27th January last, after a short illness (supposed to be influenza) at his residence in Jackson county, Georgia, in the 77th year of his age, COL. WILLIAM PENTICOST... (long eulogy)

Died at his father's residence in this place, on the morning of the 18th inst. at about 2 o'clock A.M., SAMUEL H. LUMPKIN, son of the Hon. Wilson Lumpkin, a member of the Junior Class of the University (with eulogy) (Athens Banner)

9 Apr 1839

Murder. On the night of the 20th ult. a man by the name of WM. B. HARPER was shot at the Washington Hotel, Vicksburg; it is thought by Mr. Tippo, the keeper of the house...

Homicide. An act of homicide was committed in our streets yesterday
afternoon. GEO. CHURCHWARD, a commission merchant, was shot dead through
the head by C.B. Churchill, a cotton broker...(Mobile Register, 20th ult.)

Died in Hillsboro, Jasper county, Ga. on the 4th of March, MRS. MARY BELL,
consort of Col. Bailey Bell, in the 62d year of her age; an orderly member
of the Baptist Church for about 19 years; leaves husband and children.
(with eulogy)

Died at his residence in Lawrenceville, Gwinnett county, on the 17th ult.,
DR. PHILO HALL, in the 54th year of his age.

16 Apr 1839
Died of inflammation of the brain on Sat. 30th March, at Georgetown, Georgia,
EDWARD F. SING, M.D., a native of Sing Sing, N.Y. (NY papers will please
publish)

23 Apr 1839
On the 20th ult. WILLIAM DANLAP. JR. was executed in the prison yard at
Williamsport, Pa. for the murder of his wife.

30 Apr 1839
A son killed by his father! A man named WM. MILLER, in Somerset county, Pa.,
has been committed to prison for killing his own son, a lad about 12 or 14
years of age. The latter was chopping wood and accidentally struck the axe
upon a stone, when the father became enraged, took up a handspike that was
near at hand, and struck him several blows, which occasioned his death in
a few minutes. (Pennsylvanian)

We learn by a private letter that MARCUS DESHA, a son of Gen. Desha, was
killed at the Port of Arkansas on the 2d inst. by Eugene Notribe. Desha
rushed on Notribe with a Bowie knife, when Notribe shot at him with a pistol,
but missed him. Notribe's brother then handed him a second pistol, with
which he shot Desha down upon the spot.

14 May 1839
We regret to learn by the Savannah papers that HON. JEREMIAH CUYLER,
judge of the Circuit Court of the United States for the district of Georgia,
died last week.

Melancholy occurrence happened at West Point, Troup county on Monday last.
Three young lads, one a son of Mr. George Reese, a son of Mr. Reese, and a
son of Mr. Norris, went to the river for the purpose of bathing. They
unfortunately ventured beyond their depth and were all three drowned.
(Columbus Enquirer, 8th inst.)

Died in this city on the 11th inst. of pulmonary consumption, MR. TITUS SKEIN,
in the 25th year of his age. He arrived here but a few days previous to
his dissolution...

21 May 1839
A man in Transylvania lately fell upon his scythe and killed himself at
the age of 120. This man, whose name was JOHN GRAZA, left a son 100 years
old, and a hopeful grandson of 80... (NY Gazette)

MR. L.B. YOUNG and MISS MARY ANN BARBER were both drowned in the Warrior river, near Tuskaloosa, Ala. on the 7th inst. by the upsetting of a boat while upon a pleasure excursion.

Death by a tiger. MR. MANUEL MARTIN, assistant surveyor in the revenue survey department, was killed by a tiger in the Neilgherry Hills on the 16th of October... (Madras US Gazette)

From the New Orleans Picayune 8th inst. Terrible steamboat disaster! Great destruction of life! The steamboat George Collier disaster. Those who dies were: T.J. SPAULDING of St. Charles, Mo.; CHAS. BROOKS, residence unknown; WM. PLAKE, of Boston, Mass.; CRISSEN HERRING of Germany; MRS. E. WEISH and two children, of New Orleans; SELEN J. BROCQUA of Poland, Ky.; JOHN IDEDA of France; DAVID J. ROSE of New Orleans; DEDERICK GROE of Germany; DEDERICK CROSS of Boston, Mass.; JOSEPH B. BOSSUEL of Boston, Mass.; JOSEPH LAWRENCE of Park Co., Ia.; PETER SMITH of New Orleans; CHARLOTTE FLETCH of England.

28 May 1839

Murder. A man by the name of HOGAN was murdered on Pinelog creek in this county on Sat. night about midnight, at his own house, by his muler, Western Jenks...Mr. Hogan was a Methodist minister. (Crossville Pioneer, 17th inst.)

Vicksburg murder. On the 29th ult. about 11 o'clock P.M. a man by the name of B. Beuman walked into the shop of a person by the name of VOGEE, who kept a doggery at the landing, and without any warning, deliberately shot him, the ball entering under the left breast, which caused his death in a few minutes.

Died in Macon on the 17th inst. FRANCES ANN, infant daughter of MRS. ANN BRADLEY, aged 15 months 22 days.

4 June 1839

Love and suicide - a distressing case. From the Saint Louis Gazette. Details of death of MR. JOHN D. BURNS, a clerk in the employ of Messrs. Chambers and Jones. Was about age 22.

Died in this city on Friday 31st ult. MRS. CATHARINE W. VAN VALKENBURGH, in the 28th year of her age.

11 June 1839

More Indian butchery. On yesterday we were favored with the perusal of a letter from a young lady in Florida to her uncle in this city, which is dated the 29th ult., and came by the Florida, from Garey's Ferry. The letter states that on the evening previous, about sunset a body of Indians surrounded the dwelling of a MR. OSTEEN, at Alligator, and shot him near his stable. He was instantly killed. An uncle of the writer's, MR. SIMEON DELL, who was in the stable, made his escape to the house. A sister of Mr. Osteen's was shot through the left side and arm, but Mrs. O. and her children fled to the nearest neighbor's house... (Savannah Georgian, 3d inst.)

Proclamation by Gov. George R. Gilmer offering $200 reward for the apprehension of William J. McMillan for murder committed on the body of CHARLES CARGILL in Muscogee county on the 27th of May 1839.

Proclamation by Gov. George R. Gilmer offering $200 reward for the apprehension of John Ray for the murder of JAMES DOOLY in Columbia county on the 19th instant.

18 June 1839

On Saturday last a most horrible murder was committed in the lower part of this country on the body of ELI HAYNES by his own brother, Charles Haynes... (Columbus Enquirer, 12th instant)

25 June 1839

A COL. PETERS of Perington, Monroe county, a few days since committed suicide by throwing himself headlong into a well. He had recently purchased wheat extensively at the west, and as the price of flour had fallen, he became so affected on account of the loss he expected to suffer that he committed the rash act. (NY Transcript)

Died in Harris county on the 10th inst. Major HARDY CRAWFORD, in the 40th year of his age, leaving a disconsolate widow and six children.

Died in Columbia, SC on Sat. evening the 12th inst., MRS. HENRIETTA J. JUHAN, in the 32d year of her age.

Died in Talbotton on the 27th May, MRS. ELIZABETH E., consort of CHARLES WYNN, Esq., and daughter of Rev. John Millinor, aged 30 years; member of the Baptist Church. (with long eulogy)

Died near Blountsville, Jones county, on Monday the 10th inst., MR. JOHN TICKNOR.

Died on Wednesday the 12th inst. of a protracted illness, Major JOHN CURITON, in the 43d year of his age.

Proclamation by Gov. George R. Gilmer offering $200 reward for the apprehension of Stephen Brumly for murder committed on the body of MARTIN COCHRAN in Cobb county on 2d May 1839.

2 July 1839

JOHN LARKIN, the mail robber, was executed in Mobile on the 21st in accordance to his sentence.

A few days since a man by the name of WM. HUX, who resided about nine miles east of Pineville, having apprehended two runaway slaves (a man and wife) the property of a Mr. John Welch, residing near Savannah, started for town in order to lodge them in the Work House, and then when about two miles from his house the negroes killed him and fled... (Charleston Courier, 20th ult.)

Died in Athens on the 21st ult. the HON. AUGUSTIN S. CLAYTON, in the 56th year of his age, formerly a Representative in Congress from this state.

9 July 1839

History of the life of CORNELIUS WILLHEMS, who was executed on Ellis Island, in New York harbor, on Friday 21st ult. for piracy and murder on board the Braganza...

16 July 1839

On Saturday G.B. MUSSELWHITE was instantly killed by a gun shot from the hand of John L. Ragsdale. A Coroner's inquest has been held over the body of the deceased, and a verdict excusing or justifying the act has been returned.

JOHN RIDGE killed. A gentleman who arrived here says the last Little Rock Arkansas Gazette, on Monday evening, from the West, informs us that a rumor was current there, when he left, that JOHN RIDGE, one of the chiefs of the Cherokee Indians, had been waylaid and shot, while on his return from the Council.

Murder by wholesale. Early on the night of the 15th June, the family of MR. WM. WRIGHT, residing in Washington county, near the Cherokee line, were disturbed by several men demanding admission...Mr. Wright and four of the children were killed...two other children had been severely wounded, and one escaped unhurt, who were found concealed on the bank of a creek near the premises... (Little Rock Ark. Gazette)

Villanous deed. The St. Augustine News on the 6th inst. has the following: The deaths of CAPT. MITCHELL and LIEUT. PUGH, as well as twelve soldiers, we learn is attributed to poison...

Died in this city on Thursday the 11th inst. THOMAS EGBERT, infant child of JEREMIAH BEALL, aged 4 weeks.

Died in Macon on the 6th inst. ROBERT W. FORT, in the 37th year of his age.

Died at his residence in Jones county suddenly of cramp cholic on the 2d inst. COL. ZACHARIAH ROWE, leaving a wife and several small children to lament his death.

23 July 1839

The suicide of a mathematical miser. On Friday morning last a Coroner's Inquest over the body of JEREMIAH HALLET, of Yarmouth, who on the 28th ult. killed himself by hanging...the deceased lived alone and was 64 the day the inquest was held... (long article - Yarmouth, Mass. Register)

Another Indian massacre. On Saturday night between nine and ten o'clock, the family of MR. CHAIRS - living about ten miles from town - were attacked by the Indians, and his wife and two children killed! (Tallahassee Star, 17th inst)

6 August 1839

MR. TIMOTHY CONKLIN, a lieutenant in the army under Washington, died at Milan, Ohio on the 4th inst., aged 96 years.

Died in this city on the 29th ult. MR. JAMES F. SLATTER, a native of Charleston, SC, but for the past 15 years a resident of this place, in the 47th year of his age.

13 August 1839

Headed Fort Gibson, July 2, 1839. Letter relating details of the murders of JOHN RIDGE, ELIAS BOUDINOTT, and old Major RIDGE...

The HON. JOHN BIRDSALL of New York and formerly a member of the Senate of that state, died on the 22d instant. Since his residence in Texas, he has filled the office of Attorney General and Chief Justice of the Republic.

A woman strangled by her own bonnet strings. An extremely dissipated, drunken and disorderly woman of the name of ELIZABETH KENCHEN, met her death on Wed. night last... (Pennsylvanian)

Died on the 29th ultimo at his residence in Randolph county, after nine days sickness of congestive fever, ASHLEY A. McMICHAEL, aged 26 years; leaves a widow and orphan child.

Died in Macon on Thursday 1st inst. after an illness of seven or eight days, JOHN WILLIAMS, Esq. He contracted his disease in the lower counties, and finding himself very ill, and desiring to be in the bosom of his family, he hastened to Macon, where he arrived exhausted with fatigue and disease, and survived only a week. Was born 10 April 1782 in Bertie county, NC from which state his father emigrated to Georgia when his son was an infant. Was for many years a citizen of Baldwin county, which county he twice represented in the Senate of the State, and subsequently was placed by the Legislature at the head of the Treasury Dept.; leaves widow and numerous family of children and grandchildren.

27 August 1839

From Concord (N.H.) Courier. JONATHAN BUTTERFIELD, Esq., of Hopkinton, late a taverner in Goffstown, not having sufficient nerve to meet the responsibilities of life, mearly stole out of existence last Monday night, by hanging himself.

The Mobile papers announce the death of HON. HENRY HITCHCOCK, a distinguished citizen of that place, and one of the most eminent jurists of Alabama. He died of the yellow fever.

MR. ZEBEDEE KENDALL, father of the Postmaster General, died at his residence in Dunstable, Mass., aged 84.

Died in this place on the morning of the 23d inst., THOMAS CROWDER, Esq., in the 66th year of his age; a native of Brunswick county, Virginia but removed to this state about 40 years since; connected with the Methodist Episcopal Church... (short eulogy)

3 Sep 1839

Fatal rencontre. On Wed. evening last a rencontre occurred in this place between MR. P. BURTON and MR. G.W. HUNT, in which both were wounded from the discharge of pistols - the former slightly, the latter fatally. (South Carolinian, 30 inst.)

Died at the residence of her mother in Monroe county, Ga. on the 10th ultimo, MISS ELIZABETH ANN PARHAM, aged 20 years. (with eulogy)

Died of bilious fever in Jasper county on the ult., MRS. TRACY HORTON, consort of Mr. John Horton, in the 39th year of her age; a pious and exemplary member of the Methodist Church for the last 23 years; a dutiful wife and kind mother; leaves husband and eight children.

Died at the residence of her father in Greene county on the 28th ult., MRS. CATHARINE B. AVARY, wife of Asa G. Avary, Esq., of Jasper county, in the 23d year of her age; leaves infant. (with eulogy)

From the Augusta Constitutionalist of 12th inst. Board of Health report on deaths from fever in that place: MRS. NEHR, native of Germany (resident); WILLIAM MOODY, resident; MRS. AARON ROFF, resident; BAZIL YOUNGBLOOD, resident; JOHN SANDIFORD, resident; MRS. JONES (mother of Priscilla), resident; MISS C. SABAL, resident; MASTER ALBERT BANTA, New York; JAMES L. WRAY, resident; MISS EMMA HARTFORD, resident; MRS. J. CALVIN, resident; S.P. TURPIN, resident; WILLIAM WRIGHT, resident; RICHARD MEREDITH, resident; MRS. A.Z. BANTA, New York; MRS. REBECCA QUISENBERRY, resident; HENRY DALBY, resident; MISS ELIZABETH HAMILTON, South Carolina; ASBURY KNIGHT, resident; JOHN STANSFIELD (Printer), Boston or New York; MRS. DEAVES, resident; MRS. GREEN, resident; DR. DENT, resident; MRS. BROOME, resident; JOSEPH ROUCHE, France; JOHN ABBOTT, unknown; FREDERICK SELLECK, resident; JAMES U. JACKSON, resident; WILLIAM THOMPSON, resident; HENRY E. PARMELEE, Connecticut; THOMAS ALLEN, resident; WELCOME ALLEN, resident; WILEY HARGROVES, resident; Death occurring in same place from other diseases: EDWARD H. BARRETT, MRS. MARY SAVAGE, MRS. MEREDITH, JAMES JOHNSON, J.C. GRIFFIN (died at Aiken), MRS. ELIZABETH PRYOR.

The Lexington, Ky. Intelligencer states that a bloody affray occurred at Richmond, Ky. on the 29th between MR. MUZZEY, principal of an Academy at Richmond, and MR. THOMAS M. STONE, merchant of that place, which resulted in the death of the latter...

From Augusta Constitutionalist of the 19th inst. Board of Health report of deaths from fever in that place: ALLEN ANDREWS, MRS. ANNA FOX, MRS. JAMES JOHNSON, RICHARD F. BUSH, THOMAS AVERELL, JAMES HAGGERTY, CAPT. WM. COLVIN, MITCHEL NELSON, MRS. STURGIS, GEORGE LARK, all residents; M.M. BROWN, Conn.; CHARLES SMITH, resident; MRS. CATHERINE ALBERT, Germany; MARTHA SCOTT, unknown; THOMAS PHILLIP, resident; C. BATTY, resident; MR. THOMAS LYON, Ireland; SARAH WASHINGTON, Resident; MRS. HART, Ireland; child of ASA SMITH, 8 years old, resident; ELIJAH GARRETT, resident; JOHN HENDERSON, resident; JOHN HART, Ireland; MRS. JANE MITCHELL, non-resident; ISAAC REIGHTER, Pennsylvania; MRS. FRAZER, A. STUTZMAN, EDWARD MARTIN, MRS. WM. HAYNES, MRS. ANN NORRELL, MRS. MARTHA TURNMAN - all residents.

Died in this city on the night of the 1st inst., MRS. LYDIA PIERCE, in the 75th year of her age; member of the Methodist Episcopal Church... (with long eulogy)

1 Oct 1839

From Augusta Constitutionalist of 26th ult. Board of Health report of deaths from fever in that place: GEORGE KING, WM. RANKIN, JOHN RILEY (Tailor), ISAAC HOUGHKIRK, DANIEL McMURPHY, MRS. CATHERINE CUSHMAN, MRS. ELIZA MONNLZ(?), MRS. MARGARET DEWAR, DR. MILTON ANTONY, another child of ASA SMITH, ROBERT DILLON, JOHN B. GUEDRON, DANIEL ROMAN, WM. ROUNDTREE, MISS FRANCES E. TURNMAN, VICTOR CLEPU(?), MISS G. TURNMAN (10 years old), all residents; MORGAN CONVART, unknown, believed New York; JEREMIAH P. MORRIS (in prison), Georgia; DERVIN'S son (6 years old), resident; RICHARD DERMONT, Ireland; EDWARD DEAVER, Maryland; WM. TUTT, resident; F. BLODGET (a child), resident; wid. L. HOOD, Wilkes, Ga.; WM. PANTON, JOHN J. SHEAR, WM. MORRIS, MRS. CROSLEY - all residents; JOHNATHAN DUNN, England.

8 Oct 1839

From Augusta Constitutionalist of 3d inst. Board of Health report of deaths: MRS. M'CREADY, WM. SAVAGE, MRS. MARY RUSSELL, MASTER JOSEPH HAINES, MASTER JOSEPH P. NELSON: MASTER ALFRED SIMONET, GEORGE CLEARY, GEORGE SWEET, WM. M. DAVIS, J.B. STEEL, JOHN MORRISON, ABSALOM FLEMMING, EUGENE GOLLY (child), GEORGE McMURPHY, MRS. ELIZABETH BLAYLOCK, MRS. CYNTHIA LAWRENCE, all residents; THOMAS DOWNING, non-resident; ELISHA PURSE, Mass.; ELIJAH DWEILE, Mass.; MICHAEL SHAVER, resident; WM. G. SCOTT, Georgia; HENRY GARDNER, resident; and BILLY COBB, negro-barber.

In our last paper we noticed the death of JEREMIAH P. MORRIS, in prison - it should have been JEREMIAH P. NORRIS.

HON. ALBERT G. HARRISON, member of Congress from Missouri, died at his residence in Fulton, in that state, on the 7th ult.

15 Oct 1839

Proclamation by Gov. George R. Gilmer offering $200 reward for the apprehension of Charles Rosignol for murder committed upon the body of THOMAS E. HARDEE in St. Mary's, Camden county, on the 30th day of August last.

Health of Augusta. Board of Health report on deaths as taken from the Constitutionalist of the 10th instant: PATRICK McGOVERN and IRA LEE, residents; JAMES COLLINS, Germany; MASTER JOHN SINDERSINE, MARY ELBERT (6 years old), HENRY O'NEAL, MISS FRANCES KING, CHARLES HART, ROBERT LYON, MRS. MARY DAUCETT, JOHN NELSON (son of Mitchell), residents; W.C. GRIMES, Georgia; MOSES DAUCETT and JOSEPH COLLINS, residents; MRS. ANN BURNS, Ireland.

Died in Athens on Sunday the 30th ult. after an illness of five days, ALFRED BYNUM CHASE, eldest son of Albon and Elizabeth Chase, aged 4 years 17 days.

22 Oct 1839

Health of Augusta. From Constitutionalist of 17th inst. Board of Health report of deaths by fever in that place: DR. ISAAC BOWEN and PHILIP DAUCETT, residents; EDWARD SNOOK, England; THOMAS McCANNA and JOHN LEWIS, residents; MRS. CAROLINE F. GUNTHER, Germany; ADELINE MARTIN (6 years old), resident.

In an affray at Americus, Sumter county, on the day after the Election,
a man by the name of JOHN DRAPER was shot through the head by a discharge
from a pistol, in the hands of Dempsey J. Justice, Esq., which caused
his death in a few hours... (Macon Telegraph, 15th inst.)

29 Oct 1839

Health of Augusta. Board of Health report of deaths from fever:
MR. JOHN SLOANE, MRS. GANTER, MR. TRIMBLE (all residents).
(Augusta Constitutionalist, 24th inst.)

Proclamation by Gov. George R. Gilmer offering $200 reward for the
apprehension of John O. Carter for murder committed upon the body of
JAMES CAUBIN on 31st August 1839 in Habersham county.

5 Nov 1839

Proclamation by Gov. George R. Gilmer offering $200 reward for the
apprehension of Wiley Hunt for murder committed upon the body of
OBIDIAH CHAPPELL on 21st September last in Harris county.

Health of Augusta. Board of Health report of deaths by fever in that place:
SIMEON WALKER, SANDERS WALKER, MRS. MARTHA SHAW, BENJ. SIMMS, LARRY HAY -
all residents. (Augusta Constitutionalist, 31st Oct)

Death of HON. THOMAS LEE occurred yesterday at 4 o'clock P.M. at a very
advanced age - we believe past 70. At time of his death he was Judge of the
District Court of the United States, and President of one of the city Banks.
(Charleston Mercury, Oct. 25)

Died in Milledgeville on Friday night the 29th ult., MRS. REBECCA PIERCE,
wife of Rev. Reddick Pierce, in the 54th year of her age; member of the
Methodist Episcopal Church; leaves husband, three daughters, three sons, a
brother and a sister.

12 Nov 1839

JOHN CHAPMAN, who was awaiting his sentence of death in our Jail for the
murder of his wife in December last, broke out on Sat. night!...He had been
respited by the Governor from the 22d March to 20th December next; and there
is little doubt that the Legislature, as usual, would have granted him a
pardon. (Macon Telegraph, 5th inst.)

The St. Louis Daily Gazette announces the death of JOSEPH M. WHITE which took
place in St. Louis on the morning of the 19th inst. at the residence of
his brother, Dr. T. White.

Health of Augusta. Board of Health report of deaths by fever: MASTER CHARLES
OGDEN, HEZEKIAH BAILY, JACOB DANFORTH, MRS. GAY - all residents.
(Augusta Constitutionalist, 7th inst.)

<u>26 Nov 1839</u>

Proclamation by Gov. Charles J. McDonald offering $200 reward for the apprehension of Lewis Johnson and William Glover for murder committed upon the body of MILTON P. GLOVER on 26th January last in Crawford county.

<u>3 Dec 1839</u>

A boy aged about 13 years, named UMPHREYS, having been arrested on suspicion of having set fire to Vicksburg and Natchez, died in the jail of the latter place, of yellow-fever on the 17th ult.

<u>10 Dec 1839</u>

Died in this city on the 1st inst. of a lingering illness, in his 38th year, MR. DENNIS A. BURKE, printer, formerly of New York, and lately of Milledgeville. He was employed in the office of this paper previous to his decease...native of the county of Galway, Ireland, and emigrated to America from Dublin in 1832; member of NY Typographical Society, Independent Order of Odd Fellows. (Savannah Georgian, 3d inst.)

<u>31 Dec 1839</u>

Melancholy event. On Thursday evening last R.H.H. YONGE, about 13 years of age, son of Wm. P. Yonge, Esq., of this city, while playing about the Cotton Press, happened to an accident truly lamentable. A large piece of timber used as a lever fell upon him breaking his leg and inflicted internally a wound which proved mortal. He died on Friday morning half past eight o'clock. (Columbus Argus, 25th inst.)

Died at Georgetown (D.C.) on the 19th inst. MRS. SUSAN DECATUR, relict of the late Commodore Stephen Decatur, of the US Navy. Was a native of Norfolk and daughter of the late Luke Wheeler...was married in 1806.

7 Jan 1840
COL. AUGUSTUS ALSTON is no more. Tribute of respect to him by friends convened at the City Hotel in Tallahassee on Wed. evening 17th Dec...

Proclamation by Gov. Charles J. McDonald offering $150 reward for the apprehension of James Shern for murder committed upon the body of JOHN KIMMEY on 9th inst. in Sumter county.

4 Feb 1840
Savannah, Jan 28. - Regret to announce the death of WM. TAYLOR, the late venerable and respected President of the Steamboat Company of Georgia...departed this life on Sunday after an illness of some duration... (Georgian)

11 Feb 1840
Fatal affray at Canton, Miss. An affray of a fatal nature occurred a few days since at Canton, Miss. between T.C. Tupper and DUVAL C. COOKE, two young lawyers of that place, which resulted in the death of the latter...

18 Feb 1840
Homicide. A man of desperate character, named JOHN WHITECOTTON, was killed in the lower part of this District on Tuesday last by the Deputy Sheriff, Mr. Z. Bates, while in the performance of his official duty... (South Carolinian, 14th inst.)

Another Indian murder in Florida. Headed St. John River, Feb. 7, 1840... details of the murder of FARSON COMELL.

Proclamation by Gov. Charles J. McDonald offering $150 reward for the apprehension of Moses Reese for murder committed upon the body of JOHN ENGLISH on 23d December 1839 in Franklin county.

25 Feb 1840
JOHN COPE was killed at the Navy Yard, Philadelphia, by the falling of a piece of timber while he was at work on the steam frigate.

Mail carriers murdered. Headed St. Augustine, Feb 16 - details of the murders of MR. JOS. GARCIA and others.

Died in Ashtabula, Ohio January 27, MRS. SIBBELL BARNES, widow of Mr. Thos. Barnes, deceased, of Middletown, Conn., aged 90 years.

3 Mar 1840
Proclamation by Gov. Charles J. McDonald offering $150 reward for the apprehension of Levi Long for murder committed on the body of WILLIAM WELLS on 16 Nov 1839 in Liberty County.

The Boston Herald states that MR. E.D. STEVENS, druggist of that city, on Tuesday night week, accidentally swallowed some Prussic acid, with which he endeavored to destroy...of an aching tooth, which destroyed his life.

10 Mar 1840

Died in Gwinnett county on the 25th ult. MRS. MARY STRICKLAND, consort of Wilson Strickland, Esq., in the 60th year of her age, and in the 40th year of church membership (with eulogy).

A brief history, by Richard M.D.J. Elliott, of the claim of the heirs of DAVID M'CULLOCH, long since deceased, in right of his wife JANE, MRS. PHEBE POLLARD, and SARAH R. JONES, heirs at law of said M'Culloch, who commanded a private armed Letter of Marque ship, called the Rattlesnake, of twenty guns, owned by himself and others, sailing out of the port of Philadelphia, during the war of the Revolution, under a commission from the Congress of the United States. (occupies five full page columns)

7 Apr 1840

Melancholy accident and culpable folly. On Saturday last a Mrs. McGilvery, residing on Second Street above Oak, took out a pistol belonging to her husband, who is absent...supposing it not loaded, she put a cap on and snapped it at a Mrs. Ennis, with a view of scaring her. It did not go off, and pursuing her amusement, she put on another cap and went to the house of MR. RICHARD RUSSELL, a neighbor...she snapped the pistol at his face and when it went off...Mr. Russell fell back into the house, and about four o'clock in the evening, expired-.. (St. Louis Republican); he leaves a wife and several children.

5 May 1840

Suicide on Monday last a Coroner's inquest was held on the body of one MOODY, who was found dead in the vicinity of the grave yard near this city. Verdict, Suicide...was gambler by profession. (Columbus Enquirer, 29th ult).

Horrible tragedy. A gentleman just from Whitesville, Harris county, has given as the following particulars of a most appalling incident. MR. THOS. SADDLER, a most worthy and industrious citizen of that place, had occasion some days since to chastise a child belonging to one of his negro men, we believe his confidential servant - on Saturday last Mr. S. found it necessary to inflict punishment on another child of the same family. The father in a sudden fit of rage, seized upon an axe and severed the head of the first child from its body - with a second blow he cleft the body of the other child, and turning upon Mr. Saddler, he instantly split his skull and caused his almost immediate death... (Columbus Enquirer, 29th ult.)

12 May 1840

Died at her residence three miles above Marion, Twiggs county, on Wed. morning the 23d instant, in the 48th year of her age, MRS. MARTHA ARRINGTON, relict of the late Thos. Arrington, Esq., of a painful and protracted illness of six months. (with long eulogy)

Died at Rossville, Ga. on the 19th inst. DAVID MONTFORT, late of Talbot county, supposed to be about 25 years of age. The deceased was attacked while travelling with pleurisy... (Chattanooga Gazette, 24th April)

9 June 1840

Died in Hall county, Ga. on Sunday the 24th ultimo, MRS. SARAH ROBERTS, wife of Col. James Roberts, of Hall county, in the 34th year of her age; an orderly member of the Baptist Church; leaves husband and eight small children.

16 June 1840
 The powder mill of MR. HILL and Son, in Westmoreland County, Pa. was recently
 blown up and both the proprietors killed.

23 June 1840
 Headed Newnan, June 16, 1840. Notice of the death of HON. WILLIAM G. SPRINGER
 who died at his residence at Rotherwood, Carroll county, on the 15th inst. at
 4 o'clock P.M.; disease was acute hepatitis.

 Announce the death of COL. THOMAS SUMTER, only son of the late Gen. Sumter of
 revolutionary memory, and father of the Hon. J.L. Sumter, now a member of
 Congress from this State. He departed this life on Monday morning 15th inst. at
 his residence near Stateburg, in the 72d year of his age; was himself many
 years a member of Congress, and subsequently Minister from the United States to
 the Court of Brazil.

 HON. ANSON BROWN, a representative in Congress from the district composed of the
 counties of Saratoga and Schenectady, died on Saturday evening at his residence
 in Ballston Spa... (Albany Journal).

 Died in Milledgeville on the 19th inst. in the 21st year of her age,
 MRS. SARAH F. KIMBALL, consort of W. Gustavus Kimball; native of Bangor, Me.
 but had resided in this place for the last 18 months; leaves husband.

 JAS. B. MULLIN was executed on the 2d inst. at New Orleans, for the murder of
 GREEN, committed in that city some time since.

14 July 1840
 The HON. WM. SMITH, formerly of South Carolina and late of Alabama, died at
 Huntsville in that state on the 25th ult. of congestive fever, aged 78 years.
 Judge Smith filled a large and honorable space in the public eye during his long
 and useful life.

21 July 1840
 Died at Tarversville, of congestive fever, on the night of 6th July,
 MRS. MARY ANN LEE, consort of Jordan W. Lee, Esq., aged 32 years; leaves a
 husband and children...Mr. and Mrs. Lee had just two weeks previously buried
 their little ELIZABETH MINERVA, aged two years.

28 July 1840
 Woodville (Miss.) Republican relates the details of the murders of DANIEL WOODARD
 and GEO. E. FRAZIER. Rewards offered for apprehension of Arad Woodard, the murderer
 of Geo. E. Frazier.

 Died in this city on the 24th inst., M. HALL McALLISTER, infant son of Alfred
 and Rebecca Horton.

 Died in this city at the residence of Joseph Stovall, Esq., JOSEPH THOMAS,
 infant son of Thomas and Camilla MOUGHON.

4 Aug 1840
 Died in Jones county on the 9th inst. of a protracted illness, MRS.TEMPERANCE
 GLOVER, consort of Wilie Glover, in the 47th year of her age; leaves husband
 and two children; member of the primitive Baptist church for several years
 preceding her death.

18 Aug 1840

THOMAS BELTON, a soldier of the Revolution reputed to be 108 years old, died a few days since at Newark (N.J.). He served six years in the army of the revolution, and enjoyed the benefit of a pension.

An old 'un. A man named FRANCIS BEAUREGUARD, of Boucherville, died on Monday week, at the Grey Nun's Hospital in Montreal, at the extraordinary age of 107 years 9 months 5 days.

1 Sep 1840

Died at Gainesville, Hall county, on the 20th August, JESSE SANFORD MOUGHON, in his 10th year, youngest son of Col. Thomas Moughon of Jones Co.

15 Sep 1840

Died suddenly at Whitesville, East Florida, on the 4th ult., JOHN W.H. DAWSON, Esq., Attorney at Law, in the 26th year of his age; native of this city; war cry heard in Florida and he entered the service as a cornet to the first company which marched under the command of Capt. Malone...in the two succeeding campaigns commanded by Gen. Nelson, he held the appointment of Adjutant. (with eulogy)

Died at Tarversville on Monday 24th instant from six days sickness of fever, ROBERT RUFFIN, only child of William M. and Joanna R. Tarver; very bright little boy of 6 years and 9 months... (with eulogy)
(The Georgia Journal, Montgomery and Tuscaloosa, Ala. papers please copy)

22 Sep 1840

Died in Sandersville, Washington county, THOMAS R. HARDIN, age 26 years. (with long eulogy)

29 Sep 1840

Died at the residence of B.B. Smith in Twiggs county, of inflammation of the brain, DR. RANSOM LINCH. He was confined but two days; member of the Methodist Episcopal Church...a dutiful son and affectionate brother and a kind husband...

13 Oct 1840

The Louisville Journal states "that on the night of the 20th of August, the house of John Robinson, of Logan county, Illinois, was struck by lightning, while the neighbors and family were attending the dying bed of Mrs. Robinson. John Robinson, Jr., of Sangamon, was killed at the bed-side of his dying mother. His sister, Ellen Jane, was severely shocked, and was considered dangerously hurt, and all in the house was more or less injured."

17 Nov 1840

Fatal rencontre. The Natchez papers of the 9th ult. contain an account of a fatal rencontre in Mississippi. Some time ago Mr. Richard Hagan, of New Orleans, was wounded in the chest by Mr. Lyle, formerly Mayor of Natchez. Mr. Hagan went up to his plantation a few days ago, the possession of which had been accorded to him by the decree of the Court. Shortly after his arrival, Mr. Lyle, accompanied by his overseer and several other persons all armed, went to meet Mr. H. on his plantation, where he was firedt at by Mr. Lyle, but without effect. Mr. Hagan returned the fire with a double barrelled gun, killing him on the spot...

Charles Cook has been convicted of the murder of MRS. MERRY, of Glennville, Schenectady county, New York, in September last, and sentenced to be hung on the 15th of December next.

Wm. P. Darnes, who killed A.J. DAVIS, late Editor of the St. Louis Argus, has been tried, convicted, and sentenced to 12 months imprisonment in the penitentiary.

Died in Milledgeville on the 28th ult., one of its oldest and most respected citizens, GEORGE R. CLAYTON, Esq., after a protracted illness. Mr. C. had been Treasurer of the state, continuous, for twenty years...

Proclamation by Gov. Charles J. McDonald offering $150 reward for the apprehension of David Puckett for the murder of ABSALOM LYLES in Bibb county on the 6th day of November...

A young man named SOPHON, formerly connected with the Argus Office, New Orleans, was killed in a duel near that city a few days since. His adversary was a Frenchman. They fought with rifles, at sixty paces, and at the first fire the ball entered Sophon's breast. He has left a widowed mother and a sister.

24 Nov 1840
   Died in Hamburg, S.C. on the 10th inst. after seven hours illness, of the most painful and afflicting kind, MRS. ELLEN M. WOODS, in the 23d year of her age. (with long eulogy)

1 Dec 1840
   Died in this city on the 17th inst. after a long and painful illness, WILLIAM J. BUNCE, a native of Hartford (Conn.), but for the last 41 years a resident of this city, aged 66 years. Mr. Bunce was among our oldest inhabitants; he came to this city in 1799, and in that year, in connection with George F. Randolph, commenced the publication of the Augusta Herald, which paper he continued connected with until 1823, when its title was changed to "The Georgia Constitutionalist,@ under which name he conducted it until 1832, when he sold out to the present proprietor. (Augusta Constitutionalist)

   Died on the morning of the 20th ult., MRS. FRANCES ADAMS, wife of Mr. James Adams, of Jasper county, aged 38 years 11 months 15 days; leaves husband and large family of children; member of Premative Baptist church, at Talling creek.

8 Dec 1840
   GEORGE R.Y. HEWS, one of the very few survivors of the Boston Tea Party, reached his 106th year on the 5th of September. He resides in the town of German Flats, in Herkimer county, at the house of his son-in-law, a Mr. Morrison. (Newark Adv.)

   Longevity. There is a man in Jackson township, in this county, says the Rockville Olive Branch, by the name of CONRAD EISLA, who was 110 years of age in March last. He was a captain in the war of the revolution, and commanded a company at the battle of Brandywine...

29 Dec 1840
   Died at his residence in Jones county on the 18th inst., MR. BENJAMIN FINNEY, in the 56th year of his age, and for the last 25 years a respectable member of the Baptist Church; leaves widow and children.

12 Jan 1841

Horrid assassination. Last night MR. EDWIN RUTHVEN EISLER, of Mr. Potter's theatrical company, was shot by some unknown person...Eisler's death was instantaneous, having been pierced with six or seven buckshot. He has a wife and child in the city of Jackson. (Natchez Free Trader, 21st ult.).

19 Jan 1841

Murder. MR. LINDSAY, a respectable clergyman of the Methodist Church, was murdered on Monday the 14th inst. near Hendersonville, Sumner county, and his body thrown into the Cumberland river, where it was found by dragging with a net. He was murdered for his money (about $300) by a man named Carroll, a citizen of Missouri. Carroll has made his escape, but a man named Johnson, a supposed accomplice, has been apprehended. (Nashville Union, 29th ult.).

WILLIAM D. JARRATT, Esq. died at his residence near this city on Wednesday the 13th inst. in the 64th year of his age. His disease is supposed to have been Angina Pectoris, a well known but fatal disease of the heart; a citizen of this place or neighborhood for upwards of thirty years. (with eulogy)

Died on the 2d of November 1840 at his residence in middle Florida, APPLETON ROSSETTER, Esq., aged 68 years 8 months. At an early age Mr. Rossetter emigrated to the South from his native place, Stonnington, Connecticut; extensively known in Georgia and Florida where he resided...a soldier in his early youth; leaves a wife and six children.

26 Jan 1841

DeKalb county, Ga. On the 6th of December last WILLIAM HARISTON, Esq. left his family in perfect health, for Augusta, and before his return three of his beloved family were silent in death. His daughter FRANCES BELINDA, after three days suffering of the inflammatory fever, died on the night of the 17th. On the 19th the infant was a corpse, and in a few hours the mother followed her two children to the world of spirits... (with long eulogy).

2 Feb 1841

The murder of ELLEN JEWETT. Robinson, the murderer of Ellen Jewett, whose trial and acquittal left a stain upon the tribunal before which he was arrained, went to Texas where he has since lost his right arm - that arm with which he planted a hatchet into the forehead of frail, but to him an unoffending girl, and with which he then applied an incendiary torch to the bed where she lay weltering in blood, thus attempting to conceal the murder by committing arson... (Alb. Jour.)

Death of the only survivor of Major Dade's command. RANSON CLARK, a soldier who belonged to the command of Major Dade, and who alone escaped, covered with wounds, to tell the bloody story, died recently at the residence of his father in York, Livingston county, New York.

9 Feb 1841

From the Savannah Georgian, 6th inst. Murder. MR. ROBERT PETTIGREW, the overseer of Maj. R. Mitchell, was murdered on Thursday night of last week by one or more of the negroes of Major M., near Sparta...Mr. P. had his skull badly fractured in two or three places by a club, which was found within forty or fifty feet of his body...

23 Feb 1841

Execution. The negro man who murdered MR. KIRKPATRICK, of Stewart county, was agreeable to the sentence of the Court hung in Lumpkin on Friday last... (Columbus Enquirer, Feb 17th)

9 Mar 1841

Murder. JOHN W. GAILHOUSE of Doylestown, Wooster county, Ohio, while attempting to eject his tenant, _____ Clark, by force, received a blow across the temple from an iron poker, which rendered him speechless and caused his death the next morning.

Died on Sunday evening January 31, in Paris in the 68th year of his age, of typhoid exhaustion after gout, DANIELL BRENT, Esq., Consul of the United States of America for Paris, and agent of American claims...

Died in this city on the 1st instant in the 56th year of his age, PETER BENNOCH, a native of Galloway, Scotland, and a resident of Augusta for 36 years, during which time he was extensively known as one of our most upright and intelligent merchants. (Aug. Chronicle, 4th inst.).

23 Mar 1841

Proclamation by Gov. Charles J. McDonald offering $150 reward for the apprehension of Beloved Kimbrough for the murder of a negro man named JOSHUA, the property of MARTHA CATO, in Hancock county on the 6th day of February last...

30 Mar 1841

Proclamation by Gov. Charles J. McDonald offering $200 reward for the apprehension of Marion Bazemore and Paulina Bazemore for the murder of a negro woman named BINA, the property of MARION BAZEMORE, in Jones county on Friday the 19th day of February last...

6 Apr 1841

Departed this life on the 11th ult. in the 57th year of her age, MRS. JANE VICKERS, consort of Nathan Vickers, of Decatur county; member of the Baptist Church. (with eulogy)

20 Apr 1841

MISS CAROLINE E.H.S. HORTON, the eldest child of Mr. John Horton, formerly of Hancock but for six years past a resident of Jasper county, when on her return from preaching on Wednesday the 7th inst. was thrown from her horse and killed instantaneously...was 22 years 2 months 20 days old. (with long eulogy)

Proclamation by Gov. Charles J. McDonald offering $150 reward for the apprehension of John T. Pinckard for the murder of GEORGE W. CARTER in Talbot county on the 27th day of February last...

27 Apr 1841

The Mobile Register of the 15th inst. announces the death of MARK TUCKER, formerly a citizen of this place. (with long eulogy).

4 May 1841

From the Athens Banner, Letter headed Centreville, Tablot county, Geo., April 15th, 1841. There was found yesterday morning, about one mile from Gordon's ferry on Flint River, near the residence of Mr. Courley, a man who was murdered, evidently with a hand hatchet, by being struck three blows on the head, and then having his throat cut on the left side with a knife...name of murdered man is HAMMOND...

11 May 1841

Murder. We learn that MR. JAMES H. WRIGHT, keeper of the Hotel in Knoxville, was shot down in that village on Sunday the 25th ultimo by a man named Israel Champion. The deceased lingered about 30 hours. Champion is in the Jail of this county, awaiting his trial at the August term of Crawford Superior Court. (Macon Telegraph)

We understand that MR. GILBERT DUDLEY, formerly of Effingham County, but who has resided in this city for two months past, was murdered near Springfield on the 20th ult. by some person or persons unknown...there was a wound in his thigh, caused by a musket ball, and several wounds about the breast, supposed to be made by a dagger. Was about 48 years of age, and has left a wife and five children. (Savannah Republican)

Fatal occurrence. Gen. LEIGH READ of this place was shot in the street on Monday morning last by Mr. Willis Alston. He expired in about 14 hours afterwards... (Florida Sentinel). Since the above was in type, it is reported here that one of the gentlemen said to have been wounded, the son of Gov. Branch, has also died.

18 May 1841

Proclamation by Gov. Charles J. McDonald offering $150 reward for the apprehension of Samuel M. Pitman for the murder of WILLIAM KEETON in Wilkinson county on the 4th instant...

25 May 1841

Suicide. A convict in the Penitentiary in this place, by the name of MATTOX, on Sunday last, while confined in his cell, cut his own throat with a shoe makers knife, and was found dead in a short time after the commission of the act.

8 June 1841

Proclamation by Gov. Charles J. McDonald offering $150 reward for the apprehension of Israel Champion for the murder of JAMES H. WRIGHT in Crawford county. He escaped on the night of the 4th inst. while in custody of the guard...

29 June 1841

Died at Marietta, Ga. on Monday evening the 15th inst., MRS. EVELINA S. ROBERTS, consort of Benson Roberts. (with eulogy)

Proclamation by Gov. Charles J. McDonald offering $150 reward for the apprehension of James Burns for the murder of McPERRY CUSHMAN in Baker county on Wednesday the 9th day of June inst...

6 July 1841

Death of Major General ALEXANDER MACOMB, the General in Chief of the US Army, occurred at half past two o'clock yesterday. His funeral will take place on Monday next at 10 o'clock A.M. Entered the service as a cornet of dragoons in 1799, and was in the military family of Alexander Hamilton; he commanded at the successful battle of Plattsburg during the war of 1812; received a gold medal from Congress for his gallantry and was appointed by President J.Q. Adams as Commanding General of the army of the United States, in place of Gen. Brown, immediately after his decease, which took place in Feb 1828...
(Madisonian of 26th ult.)

Atrocious murder. On Wednesday the 9th inst. a fellow names James Burns shot McPERRY CASHMAN, near the residence of Jesse Cox, Esq., in the 8th District of Baker county. The gun was charged with buck-shot, which entered Cashman's side, and from which he expired in about four hours...

Died in this city on Friday evening last after a short illness, WILLIAM S. MITCHELL, Esq., Clerk of the Superior Court of this county; eldest son of the lat Gov. Mitchell.

13 July 1841
Lengthy obituary of GENERAL MACOMB - not copied because it would appear in standard biographical sources.

Died in this city on Thursday 8th inst. RICHARD H. SANFORD, second son of Gen. John W.A. Sanford, in the 14th year of his age, in consequence of a stab in the breast, inflicted with a knife a few days before by a fellow student at Midway School...

Died at his residence in Baldwin county on the night of the 4th inst., CAPT. JAMES BONNER, of a pulomary disease which had afflicted him for the last eight or nine months... (Standard of Union)

Headed Pilatka (Florida) July 7, 1841. Announcement of the death of 2d Lieut. J.R.H. LANCASTER of the 1st Infantry, who was struck by lightning on the 5th inst. at Chrystel river, while standing in the stern of a sail boat and instantly killed.

20 July 1841
Died in Wilmington, N.C. on the 11th of June of congestive fever, MR. LEVI HART, formerly of Greenville, Ga., on his way to Southington, Connecticut.

Departed this life on Friday the 2d inst. WILLIAM S. MITCHELL, Esq., eldest son of the late Gen. David Brydie Mitchell, former Governor of Georgia; graduated at Franklin College in 1810; in 1811 he accompanied Mr. Elliott as Mathematician to the work of determining the boundary line between the states of North Carolina and Georgia, and aided him materially in ascertaining the 35th parallel of North latitude; in 1812 he accompanied the Republican Blues of Savannah under the command of Capt. Alfred Cuthbert to Florida to aid the Patriots; in 1814 was regularly admitted to the Bar in this circuit before his Honor Stephen W. Harris; in 1818 he received from his father the appointment of assistant Agent of Indian affairs in the Creek Nation; in 1819 he received from Gen. Andrew Jackson the appointment of Adjutant to the friendly Indian forces engaged in war with the tribes of lower Creeks and Seminoles, with the rank and pay of Major in the US service; from about 1820 he remained in private life engaged in agricultural pursuits until 1835, when he was elected to the office of Clerk of Superior Court of this county, which situation he continued to fill up to the period of his decease.

From the Floridian of the 10th inst. Died in Leon County on the 1st inst. ROBERT RAYMOND REID, Esq., aged about 52 years; had been a member of Congress from Georgia, a Judge of the Superior Court, Judge of the Court of Oyer and Terminer for Augusta; was appointed Judge for the Superior Court for the Eastern District of Florida during the administration of Mr. Adams, which office he held until he resigned it to accept the appointment of Governor of Florida under Mr. Van Buren...

27 July 1841

Murder. A murder was perpetrated in this city on Friday last by a Shoemaker named James Terry, on the body of a fine boy about 12 years of age, the son of Terry's present wife by a former husband. It took place in the afternoon and the boy died during the succeeding night. The child's skull was battered with a heavy stone in a shocking manner...this is the same Terry who also killed his former wife and was acquitted on the ground of insanity... (N.C. Standard)

HON. RICHARD G. DUNLAP, late secretary of the treasury of the Republic of Texas, died at New Orleans on the 22d. He was a native of Tennessee.

From the Lynchburg (Va.) Republican, 15th inst. Ward's bridge, Pittsylvania co., July 8, 1841. Awful casualty. Four persons killed by lightning. Details of the deaths of MR. WM. H. LIPSCOMB and three negroes by lightning on Wed. evening last on the plantation of Mr. Green...Mr. L. was in the 29th year of his age; a member of the Methodist Episcopal Church for ten years; left and aged father and mother residing in Charlotte county, Va.

From the Floridian of July 17th. Died at Blackwood, in this vicinity, on the 6th instant, MISS ROSALIE RAYMOND REID, daughter of the late Robert Raymond Reid, aged 22 years... (with eulogy)

3 Aug 1841

Died in Baldwin county on the 27th ult. of congestive fever, MR. ALLEN STEPHENS, in the 23d year of his age. (with eulogy)

10 Aug 1841

From the Columbus Enquirer, 4th instant. More murder. Talbot County, July 28, 1841. A highly respectable young man named EDWARD CAVENAH was shot last night, and survived but a short time. The perpetrator of this crime is supposed to be a woman...was a member of the Methodist Church.

MRS. PRISCILLA TENNILLE, consort of Col. William A. Tennille, departed this life at Palmyra, Lee county, on the morning of the 27th ult. in the 50th year of her age, and in two short days after, on the morning of the 29th ult., at the same place their beloved daughter and only offspring, MRS. WINNIFRED H. PATTERSON, in the 27th year of her age, consort of Col. Josiah Patterson, followed her mother. (long eulogy). (Standard of Union)

Died at his residence near this place on Wednesday the 4th inst., COL. SAMUEL ROCKWELL; for many years a leading member of the bar; was buried with Masonic and Military honors.

Coroner's inquest. On Thursday last an inquest was called on the body of JAMES MURRAY, who had died suddenly the day previous at the Globe Hotel. The deceased it seems had just arrived from Burke county, the place of his late residence. The jury found that he had died by the "visitation of God."

17 Aug 1841

Died in Twiggs county Aug. 10th after a painful illness of 24 days, SUSAN AUGUSTA, aged 2 years 6 months - daughter and only child of MRS. SUSAN and MR. HARDING T. SMITH. (with long eulogy)

Death of FERGUS McIVOR PATTERSON, son of Col. Josiah S. Patterson, and grandson of Col. William A. Tennille, aged 1 year 8 months 11 days - took place on the 15th instant in this city. Thus has the grandmother, mother and child paid the great debt of nature in less than one month.

24 Aug 1841

Rev. DR. BRECKINRIDGE departed this life on the 4th inst. at the residence of his mother, in Kentucky. (Presbyterian) Dr. B. was President elect of Oglethorpe University.

Proclamation by Gov. Charles J. McDonald offering $150 reward for the apprehension of Reddin J. Loyless for murder of JOHN BROWN in Cass county on the seventh day of July last...

31 Aug 1841

DR. CHARLES E. HAYNES died in this place at the residence of his brother, Col. Thos. Haynes, twnety minutes before 1 o'clock, on Sunday morning last, in the 58th year of his age; native of Virginia, but camse as a member of his father's family at a very early age to this state; represented the people of this state in Congress of the United States; member of the Methodist Church...

Tribute of Respect on Major EGBERT B. BEALL (of the city of Augusta) who died at the house of Col. Thornton in Gainesville, Hall county, on the morning of the 18th of August. His remains were carried to Monroe, Walton county, and interred...

7 Sep 1841

Died on the 26th July last at the residence of Capt. Shadrach McMichael in Jasper county, JOHN McMICHAEL, SR., aged 78 years; for last ten or twelve years a member of the Baptist Church; has left an only son with other mounring relations...

14 Sep 1841

Fatal affray. A rencontre took place this morning on the steps of the Custom House between A.H. Gazzam and COL. JOHN H. OWEN, which resulted in the instantaneous death of the latter from a stab in the pit of the stomach.

Died in Whitesville, Harris county, Ga. on the 29th of August, ROBERT WILLIAM TAYLOR, son of Wm. B. Taylor, in his 18th year...

The victims of death who are the subjects of this notice were the only daughters of Col. James and Liddle of the county of Floyd. ISABELLA JANE REBECCA departed this life on the 13th ult. in the 7th year of her age - and on the 15th ult., ESTHER ELIZABETH ADELINE, in the 13th year of her age.

21 Sep 1841

From the Cassville Pioneer, Sept 10th. Most horrid murder. The most atrocious murder that ever disgraced the annals of crime was committed on the 3d inst. in the lower edge of Cherokee county, near the Cobb line, upon the body of MRS. NANCY REYNOLDS by her own husband, Gallant Reynolds (called Runnels)...

Proclamation by Gov. Charles J. McDonald offering $150 reward for the apprehension of Gallant Reynolds for the murder of NANCY REYNOLDS in Cherokee county on the third day of September instant.

Died in this city on Thursday last, the 16th inst., GILES SPENCER, infant son of William S. and Rebecca Rockwell, aged 2 years 3 months 23 days.

28 Sep 1841

Died at his residence in Randolph county on the 12th inst. of congestive fever, DR. SMITHFIELD MARTIN, in the 27th year of his age.

Died in Wilkinson county on the morning of the 23d instant, GEORGE FRANCIS, eldest son of Henry F. and Susan A. Ruker.

5 Oct 1841

From the Boston Morning Post Extra, Sept 20. Awful murder of a young woman. Yesterday afternoon a most fiendlike murder was committed in the Cambridge alms-house (Cambridgeport) on the person of a young woman named SARAH STEVENSON by a man named William H. Britton. He plunged a huge carving knife in between her right fore-shoulder and breast, clear through her heart and lungs, and out under her left shoulderblade...

Died on the 22d of September at New Echota, Cass county, Ga., DR. H. RADCLIFF, of nervous fever, after an illness of ten days.

12 Oct 1841

Died at his residence in Russell county, Alabama on the 22d ult., DR. EZEKIEL E. PARK, in the 31st year of his age; was a native Georgian, and had for the last six years resided in Alabama; leaves a wife and five children.

Died in McDonough, Henry county, on the 3d inst., PATRICK BYRNE, a native of Dundalk, county of Louth, Ireland, but for the last twenty years a resident of the United States.

$500 reward for apprehension of Mason E. Lanier and John Lanier for the murder of JOHN E. JERNIGAN in the village of Greensboro, Ga. on Monday night the 5th inst. Signed by Albert Jernigan and Seaborn Jernigan - Greene county, Oct. 8, 1841.

19 Oct 1841

HON. ARCHER AVARY, Senator elect from Columbia county, died at his residence on Sunday last after a short but severe illness. (Chronicle & Sentinel, 12th inst

Proclamation by Gov. Charles J. McDonald offering $300 reward for apprehension of Mason E. Lanier and John Lanier for the murder of JOHN E. JERNIGAN in Green county on Monday the 4th inst.

26 Oct 1841

Died in Twiggs county Oct 6th of congestive fever in the sixt year of her age, LAURENIA EUDOCIA, daughter of Mr. Silas and Mrs. Martha Brown. (with long eulogy)

Death of MRS. JOANNA RUTHERFORD TARVER, aged just 40 years, consort of Mr. Wm. M. Tarver, and last daughter of old Mrs. Slappey. She died at Tarversville, Twiggs co., Ga. between 1 and 2 o'clock on Saturday night, 29th of August last, after a severe illness of 25 days... (long eulogy)

16 Nov 1841

Died at her father's residence in Washington Co. on the 31st Oct. of congestive fever, MISS EUNICE ANN, daughter of David Greer, Esq., in the 22d year of her age, leaving her fond parents, sisters and many friends and relations to mourn their loss... (with long eulogy)

Died in Washington county on the 27th Oct., after a protracted illness of four weeks, ALEXANDER THOMPSON, aged just one year, infant son of Roger and Harriet Thompson.

23 Nov 1841

$100 Reward. MR. LITTLEBERRY HOLLINGER who died in June 1840, I am informed that some few minuted before the breath left him, stated he had made and recorded a DEED to me for a certain negro woman, and her increase; any clerk of the courts of Georgia or Florida, who can find a title on record to me, of said property...Hollinger has resided in Burke, Laurens and Early counties, Georgia, and in Gadsden county, Florida. Signed Thomas Speight, Blakely, Early county, Ga. Sep. 6, 1841.

21 Dec 1841

ROBERT CUNNINGHAM, Esq., a highly respectable and wealthy planter of Jefferson County, was on Tuesday last murdered by his negroes...

25 Jan 1842

$300 Reward. A base murder was committed in the county of Upson, Ga., on Monday night the 3rd inst., on the body of CHRISTOPHER CONNER, by a man named Simeon Jay, and he having fled from justice...signed Sarah M.W. Conner.

8 Feb 1842

The HON. LINN BANKS, for many years Speaker of the House of Representatives of Virginia, and late Rep. in the United States Congress, was recently drowned, in attempting to cross Conway river, on his return home from Green Court House.

15 Feb 1842

Death of Judge HOPKINSON. This venerable jurist and citizen of Philadelphia died of apoplexy a few days since. He was the author of the popular national air - "Hail Columbia."

22 Feb 1842

Died in Edgefield, S.C. on Sunday the 27th ult., in the 25th year of his age, MR. EDMUND A. GLASCOCK, of Milledgeville, Geo., son of the late Gen. John Glascock, of this state; a native of South Carolina, where he spent most of his life till the last ten years; in spring 1836 served as volunteer for the Florida service; appointed secretary to Gov. McDonald...

1 Mar 1842

Death of DR. VAUGHAN. A letter recived in Richmons says that Dr. Vaughan, who shot young Pleasants at the Columbian Hotel, some three years ago, was killed recently in Texas. Vaughan went to cowhide a young carpenter, formerly of Richmond, for some expressions that were used at a public meeting; and as Vaughan collared him, the young man seized a hatchet and clift his skull to the brain, killing him outright.

8 Mar 1842

Departed this life December 20, 1841 in Anson county, N.C. after a short but severe illness, the REV. ELIJAH SINCLAIR, of the Methodist Episcopal Church, and member of the Georgia Conference, but recently a merchant of Savannah; has left a helpless widow and several orphans.

15 Mar 1842

Horrible tragedy. By a slip from the Southport Telegraph, Wisconsin, we learn that the HON. CHARLES C.P. AVANT, member of the Council from Brown county, was shot dead, on the floor of the Council chamber, by James R. Vinyard, member from Grant county. The affair grew out of a nomination for Sheriff for Grant county...

Fatal affray. A quarrel had taken place some short time previous between MR. THOMAS HUTCHINSON and a MR. McMILLAN, an engineer on the Georgia Rail Road... the result of which was that both went armed for a meeting, which took place in Broad street about 11 o'clock on Monday night, when McMillan accosted and assaulted Hutchinson, a short fight ensued, in which Hutchinson stabbed McMillan, of which he died in a few minutes... (Augusta Sentinel).

The Hon. LEWIS WILLIAMS, a Representative in Congress from North Carolina, died on Tuesday 22 ult. of bilious pleurisy, after an illness of twenty-four hours. His remains were yesterday interred at the Congressional burial ground.

Died at Fort Gaines, Ga. on the morning of the 4th instant, MR. ANDREW J. KIRKLAND, a native of Washington, Wilkes county, Ga., in the 26th year of his age.

22 Mar 1842

Hydrophobia - A most dreadful and fatal case. A fatal case of this malady has just occurred at Lafayette, which is thus reported in yesterday evening's Louisiana American...MR. G.S. JOHNSON was a native of Norfolk, Virginia... a mason by trade, and has left a wife and eight children.

Singular fatality. The following account of an afflicting dispensation of Providence that recently occurred at Nelson, Portage county, Ohio, is from the Ohio Star: On the 3d inst. an only child of MR. STEWART HOTCHKISS died after a protracted illness. On the 7th inst. Mr. H. himself was killed by the fall of a tree near his house, while engaged in chopping...

Suicide. MR. ALEXANDER RUSSEL, a citizen of Macon, committed suicide on the 16th by taking prussic acid; has left a wife and seven children.

Died March 7th at his residence in Marion, Twiggs county, JAMES SOLOMAN, Esq. in the 42d year of his age; born in Montgomery county, and at an early age, his father brought him to Twiggs county...leaves wife and children (eulogy).

Proclamation by Gov. Charles J. McDonald offering $150 reward for the apprehension of Spencer Hudgins for the murder of SOLOMON HADDER in Forsyth county on the 8th day of February last...

29 Mar 1842

Departed this life in this place on Friday morning a few minutes past nine o'clock, after a lingering illness, MRS. NANCY GODWIN, aged 40 years. (with long eulogy)

Died at the residence of her sister, Mrs. Rogers, in this city, on Wednesday morning last, MISS SARAH ANN SCOTT, aged about 40 years...

19 Apr 1842

Death of BISHOP ENGLAND (Roman Catholic). He breathed his last about 5 o'clock yesterday morning after a protracted and painful illness, in the 56th year of his age. Was a native of Ireland, and for the last 22 years resided in this city - during which period he presided over the Diocese comprising the states of North Carolina, South Carolina and Georgia... funeral obsequies will be celebrated at the Cathedral of St. Sinnhar at 10 o'clock AM this morning... (Charleston Courier, 12th inst.)

10 May 1842

The Right Rev. Bishop CONWELL departed this life on Thursday evening last at an advanced age. This venerable prelate of the Catholic Church had been afflicted by blindness for many years prior to his decease. (Philadelphia Inquirer, 24th inst.)

Distressing accident. A young man named ADAM CROFT, whilst riding from Winchester to his home in Carroll county, was thrown from his horse, one foot sticking in the stirrup. He was dragged in this position for some time... being so dreadfully bruised and mangled he only survived a few hours. It is a strange coincidence that this young ma's father was killed in a similar way, a short time previous.

Singular death of a thief. A young man named JACOB PAINE met his death near Georgetown, D.C. on Friday last. It appears that the deceased was attempting to rob the poultry house of a man named Gillum... (Philadelphia Chron.)

MR. ROBERT S. ALLEN, a highly respectable citizen of Troup county, with his nephew a lad, and three negro boys were drowned in the Chattahoochee near Hathorns Ferry, Troup county, on Saturday 23d ult...

17 May 1842

The body of LIEUT. BORDEN, of the steam-frigate Missouri, was brought to Washington and interred in the congress burying ground on Monday.

Death of HINES HOLT, SR.; native of Virginia; removed to Georgia in
1797 and continued to reside there until within two or three years of his
death...removed to Russell county, Alabama and died on his farm in that
county on Saturday evening about 4 o'clock in the 72d year of his age; for
upwards of forty years a zealous member of the Methodist Church. (Argùs)

Died in Macon on Sunday evening 8th inst., MRS. ADELINE M. FORT, aged 43,
relict of the late Mr. Robert W. Fort, of that city.

Died in Macon on Sunday morning 8th inst. of a pulmonary affection to
which he had been several years subject, MR. HAMILTON ATCHISON, of Lexington,
Kentucky, aged about 40 years; extensively known in this state, which he had
annually visited as a drover for many years; his remains, at his own request,
will be removed to Ketuaky, to be deposited in the family vault.

24 May 1842

Tattnal Co. April 28, 1842. On Sunday evening 24th inst. MR. JOSIAH ALEXANDER
and his wife, in returning home from a short visit to the house of one of
their neighbors, having the Ohoopy river to cross...getting in a strong current
of water; by which event his wife was drowned and he himself narrowly
escaped...

Departed this life on the morning of the 17th instant after a long protracted
illness with consumption, MRS. ELIZABETH A. CROWDER, relict of the late
Thomas Crowder, Esq., in the 68th year of her age; native of Orange county,
N.C.; for 33 years a consistent member of the Methodist Episcopal Church.

Died in Roxbury, Mass. on the 7th instant, HIRAM ADAMS, printer, aged 25,
formerly of New Hampshire.

31 May 1842

From St. Augustine Herald, 20th inst. More Indian murders. The mail of Wed.
brought us tidings of five more murders by the Indians in Columbia and
Alachua counties on the 14th and 15th inst. On the 14th Messrs. William
and BRYAN VANSANT, in company with Mr. A. Osteen, while hunting were attacked
by a party of thirty Indians, who shot Mr. Vansant dead from his horse...on
the 15th the same party, it is believed, attacked the house of MR. MOSES CASON
in Alachua county, killed his wife and infant child...

7 June 1842

Died in Henry county, Ga. on the 23d ult., MARTIN VAN BUREN GARRETT, infant
son of William Garrett, Esq., aged 1 year 27 days.

14 June 1842

Died at his father's residence in Twiggs county on the 31st day of May,
WASHINGTON, eldest son of JOHN FITZPATRICK, Esq., in the 9th year of his age.

Departed this life on Friday the 10th instant, THOMAS THADEUS, youngest son
of William and Lucy Jameson, on Monroe county, aged 1 year 6 months 29 days.

5 July 1842
>We have the melancholy duty of announcing the death of
HON. WILLIAM S. HASTINGS, an estimable and highly respected
member of the House of Representatives from the state of
Massachusetts. He died a few days ago at the Sulphur Springs,
of Virginia, whither he had gone for the benefit of his health,
which had for some time previously been in a declining state.
(Nat. Intel. 27th ult.)

>Died in Twiggs county on the 23d instant, MASSEY GILDON, infant
son of Charles Gildon, junior, aged 9 months 1 day.
(Savannah Geo. please copy)

19 July 1842
>Departed this life on the 6th inst. after a protracted illness of
21 days, LEVIN DORMAN, son of Wm. J. and Harriet H. SMITH, aged
11 months 3 days (short eulogy).

>Died in Pulaski county on the 10th inst. from inflammation of the
brain, LEONIDAS JAMES AUGUSTUS, son of Col. Burwell and Mrs. Lavinia
JORDAN, aged 12 months 27 days.

>Died at his residence in Washington county on the 12st June,
ROGER LAWSON, in the 28th year of his age, leaving behind a wife
and two little children... (short eulogy)

>Died in Savannah on the 9th inst. of paralysis, COL. JOHN T. LAMAR,
of Macon, Ga.

26 July 1842
>Died on Monday evening the 18th inst. at his residence near Darien,
COL. E.S. REES , formerly Cashier of the Bank of Darien.

2 Aug 1842
>Died at Gainesville, Sumpter county, Ala. on 28th June, MRS. SUSAN
BOHANNAN, consort of Mr. Young Bohannan, and daughter of the late
James Wade of Morgan county, Georgia, aged about 55 years. Also at
the same place on 30th June, MR. YOUNG BOHANNAN, a native of Georgia,
aged about 65 years. Mr. and Mrs. Bohannan were among the oldest
settlers of the State of Ala. having emigrated from the State of
Georgia to that country at a very early period of its settlement,
where they resided upwards of twenty years...had lived together in
a married state about 40 years...Mrs. Bohannan had been for long
period prior to her death a member of the Baptist Church.

>Died in Lumpkin, Stewart county, on Sat. the 25th of June last, at
the residence of her brother-in-law, Matthew Wright, Esq.,
MISS EMELIA E. PERRY, in the 23d year of her age; member of the
Methodist Episcopal Church (long eulogy).

9 Aug 1842

Departed this life on 12th July 1842, in the full triumphs of Gospel faith, MISS SARAH EMELINE GREER, in her 20th year, daughter of David and Rebecca Greer, of Washington county; had been an acceptable member of the M.E. Church at Zoar, Sandersville circuit, for about 18 months; leaves an afflicted father... (with eulogy)

Departed this life on 16th July 1842, MISS ELIZABETH F. GREER, in the 17th year of her age, daughter of Mr. David and Mrs. Rebecca Greer, of Washington county. (with eulogy).

23 Aug 1842

Murder. We learn that a man by the name of ELIJAH HOLLY was murdered in Pulaski county some time last week by another man named Arthur Mock; they were both residents of said county; a personal recontre had previously taken place, in which Mock was worsted. A few days after the recontre, Mock waylayed Holly in the woods and shot him as he was passing along the road, and immediately fled. Mock is much advanced in years; but Holly was a young, stout, and strong man.

Departed this life in Russell county, Alabama, on Saturday 30th July after and illness of two days and a half, of congestive fever, WILLIAM MOSELY, fourth son of Albert G. and Mary BECKHAM, aged 10 years 4 months 23 days.

Died on Monday first day of August after three days illness of congestive fever, LINNAEUS GILBERT LAFAYETTE, fifth son of Albert G. and Mary BECKHAM, aged 7 years 1 month 6 days.

30 Aug 1842

Fatal rencountre. On Sat. evening (says the Augusta Chronicle of the 22d inst.) a difficulty occurred in Hamburg, between Mr. Joseph Woods and MR. JAMES ROONEY, in which the latter received a wound from a pistol shot, of which he died in a few minutes. We learn that Mr. W. considers himself so fully justified that he will deliver himself to the legal authorities.

A most melancholy accident has happened to a beautiful and interesting little girl, just ten years old, on the fourth of July last, NANCY ADALINE BOWEN, daughter of William and Frances Bowen; Bowensville, Irwin Co...died from the fall of a tree. (long article with details)

6 Sep 1842

Died in this place on the morning of the 4th instant, in the 16th year of her age, MISS MARTHA, daughter of Col. David ROSS, of Putnam county...just introduced as a member of Dr. Cotting's school.

Died at Palmyra, Lee county, on the 27th of August last, LAURA VICTORIA, only daughter of John S. and R.H. MARLIN, aged 3 years 2 months 23 days.

13 Sep 1842

Proclamation by Gov. Charles J. McDonald offering $150 reward for the apprehension of Nathaniel Crenshaw for the murder committed upon the body of RICHARD BURNETT in Cobb county on the third instant...

Proclamation by Gov. Charles J. McDonald offering $150 reward for the apprehension of Arthur Mock for the murder committed upon the body of ELIJAH HOLLY in Pulaski county on the 26th of July 1842...

20 Sep 1842

Another Rev. pàtriot gone! Departed this life on the 14th of June last, in the county of Franklin, where he had resided for the last 42 years, JAMES MARTIN, Esqr., in the 83d year of his age.

Died at his residence in Richmond county on the 10th inst. of billious fever, ABSOLAM RHODES, Esq., in the 72d year of his age, after an illness of nine days.

Died in this city on the morning of the 19th inst., MARY ANN ANDERSON, infant daughter of Mr. and Mrs. A.M. HORTON, aged 1 year 1 month 23 days.

27 Sep 1842

Announcement of the death of MRS. LETITIA TYLER, wife of the President of the United States.

4 Oct 1842

Died at his residence in Baldwin county on the 11th of August last, BASDALE P. MILLER, in the 64th year of his age; was afflicted for the last two years of his life with jaundice and dropsy of the chest; member of the Baptist Church for the last thirty years of his life (with eulogy).

Died at the house of Mr. Isaac Newell in this place on Sat. morning last, MR. ROYAL SAMUEL HALL; native of Conn. and a member of the Presbyterian Church in the place of his former residence... (with eulogy)

Died in Savannah on the 27th ultimo, MR. N.D. TREANOR, a native of Tyrone county, Ireland, but for the last ten years a resident of the United States, the last part of which he spent in Milledgeville as a Merchant.

11 Oct 1842

Execution for murder. We understand that JAMES SWETMAN, who was convicted at the last term of the Superior Court of Jackson county, of the murder of MR. WHITE, some time in May, underwent the sentence of law at Jefferson on last Friday. (Athens Banner, Oct 7th)

Indian murder. MRS. CHARLOTTE CRUM, wife of Richard R. Crum, was the name of the lady killed by Indians on 12th ult. near Chuckahattee. The Indians cut off her head. We learn from the St. Augustine News that Mr. McDonald, who was driving the carriage which contained Mrs. Crum and the little girl, received a severe wound but made his escape by concealing himself in a hammock. Mrs. Hern, who was riding on horse back about fifty yeard ahead of the carriage, succeeded in taking her daughter up on the horse and made her escape whilst the Indians were murdering Mrs. Crum.

Died at Smithfield, near Sparta, MARY SMITH, daughter of Dr. William P. HAYNES, of Sandersville, aged 8 years 2 months.

25 Oct 1842

Execution in Lumpkin county. On Friday last the execution of HAMILTON SNEAD, convicted of the murder of HUGH CAMPBELL about a year since in Dahlonega, took place near that village... (Athens Banner, 21st inst.)

Died on the 26th ult. at the residence of Jesse Rambo in Gwinnett county, JOHN M. THOMPSON of Chattooga county, long known as a merchant in Lawrenceville.

Died at her father's residence near Lawrenceville on the 1st ult. of Dropsy, MISS EUNICE M. PITTMAN, daughter of Maj. Daniel N. Pittman, in the 14th year of her age.

1 Nov 1842

Another Rev. hero has bade us farewell. Died at his residence in Jones county on the 18th Oct 1842 the venerable citizen and patriot JOHN LAMAR, Esq., in the 81st year of his age... (very long obituary)

Died in Campbell county on the 20th of Sep last, SOLETHA SUMMERLIN, the wife of Joseph Summerlin, in the 29th year of her age; leaves a companion and four small children...

8 Nov 1842

Died at Midway on Wed. evening last, MR. CYRUS JONES, aged about 40 years, formerly of Wilton, New Hampshire. Mr. Jones' death was occasioned by being thrown out of a wagon... (New Hampshire papers please copy)

ORREN D. WHITAKER of Cusseta, Alabama, formerly of Georgia, died on the night of the 26th ult. at his residence after a short but painful illness, aged between 45 and 50 years...endeared to a doating wife and numerous children...orderly member of the Baptist Church.

Died at her residence on the morning of the 31st of October, MRS. ORAH AVERY, in the 69th year of her age, and for 34 years a resident of Jasper county; member of Baptist Church (short eulogy).

15 Nov 1842

Proclamation by Gov. Charles J. McDonald offering $100 and/or $300 reward for the apprehension of One/all of the suspects (William Vaughn, George Tucker, Benjamin T. Vaughn) who are accused of the murder of LEWIS, a slave, in Jasper county on the 18th of October last...

22 Nov 1842

GEORGE W. LORE, the convicted murderer of HENRY BLAKE, somewhat notorious for the ferment in which he kept the good people of Barbour county, Ala. last year, has at last been taken and has experienced the penalty of the law... (Montgomery Advertiser)

Died at his residence on the evening of the 2d inst., MR. NOAH BUTT, aged 66 years 2 months 25 days, and for 33 years a citizen of Jones county (with eulogy).

Departed this life at Bellview, Talbot county, Ga. on the morning of the 12th Nov. CINCINNATUS D., infant son of Cincinnatus D. and Emelina A. CRITTENDEN, aged 7 months 13 days.

Died in Hawkinsville on the 7th inst. of Billious fever, SARAH JANE, daughter of B.W. COLLIER, Esq., aged 7 years 16 days.

29 Nov 1842

Proclamation by Gov. Charles J. McDonald offering $150 reward for the apprehension of Bennett Weaver for murder committed upon the body of SHEPHERD W. RILEY in Muscogee county on 9 Nov 1842.

6 Dec 1842

Departed this life at his residence in Warrenton, Ga. on Tuesday morning 22d Nov., STARLING JONES, Sen'r. Was born near the High Hills of Santee, SC 21 Sep 1769, and at about age 12 or 13 moved with his parents to Georgia, and then returned to his native state. At about his 17th year he returned to Georgia and resided in Warren county until his death...had acquired a considerable estate by which he had raised a lareg family...
(The Georgia Argus and Augusta Constitutionalist please copy)

Died in Macon county on 25th October last, ABSALOM MYERS, Esq., aged 74 years; a worthy and acceptable member of the Baptist Church.

Died in Macon on the 26th ult., COL. DAVID RALSTON, a native of South Carolina, but a citizen of Georgia since 1809, aged 48 years - one of the original founders of that city.

Another patriot of '76 gone. Died at the residence of Henry Finney in Jones county on the 2d Nov, DANIEL REYNOLDS, in the 81st year of his age, after an illness of 15 days; was a native of South Carolina and emigrated to Georgia during the struggle for liberty between the Colonies and Great Britain...

13 Dec 1842

Died at his river plantation in Monroe county, Ga. on the morning of the 27th ultimo, Major JAMES W. TINSLEY, aged 55 years; native of South Carolina; member of Methodist Episcopal Church. (Macon Telegraph and SC papers copy)

Notice of the death of HON. RICHARD W. HABERSHAM - occurred on Friday last, the second instant, at his residence in Habersham county...
(Augusta Chronicle, 7th inst.)

13 Dec 1842 - Extra

The Arkansas Intelligencer of the 11th ult. mentions the death of Ex-Gov. MONTFORT STOKES, of N. Carolina. He died at Fort Gibson, Arkansas on the 4th ult. in the 82d year of his age. At time of death he was Indian Agent for the Cherokees.

Death has again been busy in the family of the late revered President Harrison. MRS. MARY S.H. THORNTON, wife of Dr. Thornton, and third daughter of Gen. Harrison, died at North Bend on the 15th inst. We believe this is the 4th child of Gen. Harrison that has died within the last three years.

20 Dec 1842

Departed this life after a short but painful struggle, MISS MARTHA CAROLINE BROWN, in the 15th year of her age, and daughter of Richmond and Martha P. Brown, of Hancock county. (long eulogy)

Died in this city on Sat. the 17th inst., ANN ELIZA, eldest daughter of
Benjamin T. and Elizabeth BETHUNE, ahed 2 years 11 months 29 days.

Proclamation by Gov. Charles J. McDonald offering $150 reward for the
apprehension of James Rooney for murder committed upon the body of
WILLIAM H. CRAWFORD in Columbia county on the 27th Nov last...

27 Dec 1842

Died at his residence in Jasper county, Ga. on the 27th October last,
MR. ELEAZAR LOVEJOY, in the 62d year of his age; member of the Methodist
Episcopal Church for 32 years; left wife and large family of children.

Died on Sat. last the Rev. DR. JAMES GRAHAM, pastor of the Roman Catholic
Church of this city, aged about 33 years.

Died in this county on the 7th inst. MR. WM. A. THARP, aged about 30 years.

Died in this city on the 17th inst. MR. MARTIN L. HARDIN, aged about
33 years. (Macon Messenger)

3 Jan 1843

Proclamation by Gov. Charles J. McDonald offering $150 reward for the
apprehension of John Kimbrough for the murder of DREWRY W. BANKSTON in
Butts county on the fifth instant...

10 Jan 1843

Died at his residence in Washington county on the 1st inst., MR. WILLIAM FISH,
in the 43d year of his age...left behind a large family. (short eulogy)

Died in Marietta on the first instant, CHARLES EUGENE, son of General Hiram
HOWARD, aged 8 years...He was induced to join some boys at play in revolving
the turntable on the Rail Road but a little distance from his father's
door. On approaching them, he was accidentally thrown upon the platform in
swift motion, and with violence forced in its revolution, between two heavy
timbers, causing immediate death.

17 Jan 1843

Proclamation by Gov. Charles J. McDonald offering $250 reward for the
apprehension of Jefferson Clay and Samuel Clay for the murder committed
upon the body of LANDON CARTER in Jasper county on the 3rd instant...

Proclamation by Gov. Charles J. McDonald offering $200 reward for the
apprehension of unknown person who committed murder upon the body of
DR. WILLIAM TAYLOR in Jones county on the 31st of December last...

31 Jan 1843

MR. T.W. WHITE, Editor of the Southern Literary Messenger, died yesterday
morning... (Richmond Compiler, 20th inst.)

Died at his residence in Decatur county, WILLIAM BLEWIT, aged 81 years.
He was a hero of the Revolution, a worthy citizen, and an esteemed patron
of the Federal Union.

14 Feb 1843

Departed this life on the morning of the 23d ult. at the residence of
Dr. Samuel Boykin, of Columbus, Ga., MISS ADELIA R. COOPER, daughter of
Hon. Mark A. Cooper of this State, aged 15 years 1 month 23 days.

Died near this city on Wednesday the 1st inst., JAMES M. COLLINS, youngest
son of David and Susan M. Collins, aged 1 year 2 months 15 days.

Died at his residence in Abbeville Dis., S.C. on the 31st ult., CAPT. JAMES
CALHOUN, in the 64th year of his age. The deceased was an elder brother
of the Hon. John C. Calhoun.

Horrid murder. A most shocking murder was committed on the body of
JOHN REA, residing in the vicinity of Greenville (Tennessee) on Thursday
of last week by his Negro man... (Greenville Mountaineer)

21 Feb 1843

Died suddenly in Jones county, Ga. on Sunday evening the 5th inst., about
3 o'clock, JAMES LOCKETT, Esq., of Clinton, Ga., aged about 55 years; an
exemplary member of the Baptist Church; leaves a bereaved widow and one
son. (short eulogy)

Melancholy occurrence. ELIJAH M. AMOS, Esq., of Knoxville, Crawford
county, was killed on Wednesday morning of last week. He was on his way
to this city, in a sulky or buggy, and when from two to three miles from
home, his horse became frightened and ran - he was either thrown or
attempted to jump from the vehicle, when he became entangled and was
dragged near a mile before he was disengaged...probably about 43 years old,
and had been a resident of Knoxville since the early settlement of the
county; for many years was Clerk of Superior Court of this county, and
Post Master at Knoxville at the time of his death. (Macon Messenger, 9th inst.)

28 Feb 1843

Fatal accident. JOHN PARKS and JONATHAN THOMAS, both of Tennessee, were
killed on last Monday, working in a mine near this place...

Tribute of respect on the death of EDWARD PAINE, Esq. by the citizens of
the county and members of the bar attending the Superior Court at
Watkinsville on Monday last.

Another Rev. soldier called to his rest. Died in this city on Tuesday
morning the 14th inst., MR. JOHN MARTIN, at the advanced age of 105 years.
Mr. Martin's parents came to this country with a party of Saltzburghers,
who emigrated under the direction of Oglethorpe, and finally removed to
the state of South Carolina, on the Congaree river, in a settlement called
the Dutch Fork, where the subject of this notice was born. He lost both his
parents at an early age, and, with an only brother was thrown upon the
world a friendless boy. Joined the Colonial Troops and served in the
Cherokee war of 1755. In an action during the campaign, he received a
severe wound in the head from an Indian tomahawk...in the Rev. War he was
with Gen. Lincoln's army when it crossed the river a few miles below Augusta;
was at the battle of Stono, in which action he lost an only brother who was
also a soldier in the Rev. army; was at the attack on Savannah - and became
a prisoner with Gen. Lincoln's army at the capitulation of Charleston; was
exchanged in time to arrive at Yorktown...a member of the Methodist Church;
his body was escorted from the church by the Richmond Hussars, Augusta Artillery
Guards and the Clinch Riflemen, followed by the Mayor and Members of the

City Council to the grave yard. (Augusta Chronicle, 24th inst.)

7 Mar 1843
Died in Marion, Twiggs county, Feb. 19th in the seventh year of his age, JONAS JACKSON, son of Mrs. Eliza & Mr. Josiah DANIEL. (eulogy)

14 Mar 1843
Horrible effects of Millerism. MR. NATHANIEL BROWN, of Kingstown, N.H., formerly travelling agent of the Exeter Mutual Fire Insurance Office, cut his wife's throat on Thursday last, in such a shocking manner that her life was despaired of. It is said he was partially deranged, caused by over-excitement on the Miller doctrine.

21 Mar 1843
Died in Coweta county on the 28th ult. of Scarlet Fever, JOSEPHINE LOUISA, only daughter of Thomas W. and Sarah Ann PATRICK, aged 1 year 3 months.

11 Apr 1843
BENJAMIN D. WHITE, recently convicted at Le Roy, Genesee county, New York, of the murder of his father, has been sentenced to be hung on the 29th of April next...

25 Apr 1843
Court martial proceedings against Commodore Mackenzie for the hanging of PHILIP SPENCER, a Midshipman... (from the Baltimore American)

Died in this place on the 20th inst., MRS. ADELINE CLARK, consort of Mr. John C.F. Clark, in the 28th year of her age; leaves a bereaved husband. (with eulogy)

2 May 1843
From the Columbus Times. On Friday last the 14th instant, at the residence of Benjamin W. Walker, Esq., at Mount Meigs, Alabama, GEN. JAMES C. WATSON of this city breathed his last, in the 56th year of his age...left Columbus about four weeks since on a visit to Alabama and was soon after seized with the same illness which terminated his life...had been in feeble health for several years...was born in Cumberland county, North Carolina and came at an early age to Baldwin county, Georgia, where he resided until 1832, when he removed to this city; served Baldwin county in either branch of the Legislature for 15 years...disease which terminated his life was inflammation of the stomach. (eulogy)

9 May 1843
Died in this city on Saturday 22d of April, MAJ. THOMAS WRIGHT, aged 49.

16 May 1843
Died in Scottsboro, near this City, on Friday last, WILEY W., son of Wiley and Mary CULLENS, in the 11th year of his life. The deceased came to his death by the accidental discharge of a pistol... (long eulogy)

From the N.J. American. Awful murder in New Jersey. $1000 reward for the murderers! Details of the murder of MR. JOHN B. PARKE (a bachelor), his brother-in-law JOHN CARTNER who worked the farm - his wife and four children - together with a servant woman - on Monday last near port Colden, Warren county, New Jersey.

78

Arrival of Admiral HORNE, the supposed murderer. This individual charged
with the murder of his wife MELINDA HORN in Baltimore county, and also a
fugitive from justice in Logan county, Ohio, where he went by the name of
Adam Hellman, and was charged with murdering a former wife about two years
ago, was brought to this city from Philadelphia...Horn formerly resided in
Loudon county, Va. (Baltimore Patriot)

23 May 1843
Another execution for murder. THOMAS J. CHAMBERS, who was convicted of the
murder of KEMP and sentenced to be hanged on Friday the 12th inst., at the
last March Term of the Superior Court of the county of Gwinnett, was
executed on that day...offence was committed in Gwinnett county some eight
or nine years ago, when he made his escape and fled to Texas - his wife
and part of his children followed him there; was arrested in Kentucky...

All for love. A young man by the name of JOHN PANCADE in McDonough county,
Illinois, recently committed suicide in consequence of the rejection of
his addresses by a young lady. Verdict of coroner's jury - death by
Susanside.

30 May 1843
Died at her son's house near Darien, MRS. SARAH SPALDING, of Sapelo Island,
aged 65 years, leaving her now aged husband after a union of 48 years...ten
children had preceded her.

Departed this life on Saturday the 27th inst., BENANUEL BOWER, Esq.,
of this city. Mr. Bower was born 27 May 1786 and was in his 57th year when
he died. For many years he was a citizen of Milledgeville.

Died at his residence in Baldwin county on the 4th inst., MR. JAMES G. RUSSELL,
a soldier of the revolution, aged 81 years.

Died on the 29th of April at his residence in Hancock county, COL. JAMES G.
LEWIS, in the 43d year of his age.

6 June 1843
A conscientious murderer...the case of Leavitt who was arraigned last week
at Plymouth, Mass. for the murder of MARY KNAPP...

An inquest was held on the 2d June instant over the body of a man named
GEORGE W. CROWDER, an escaped convict from the Georgia Penitentiary, and
the Jury returned a verdict that the deceased came to his death by a blow
or blows inflicted on the left side of his head by one or more of Wm. Sanford's
negroes, while in the act of arresting said Crowder, on the 31st day of May.

13 June 1843
Proclamation by Gov. Charles J. McDonald offering $300 reward for the
apprehension of person or persons unknown who committed murder upon the body of
WILEY GUDGER, a Penitentiary guard, in Twiggs county on the sixth instant...

20 June 1843

> Killed instantaneously on Wednesday, 2 o'clock P.M., 7th instant,
> at the residence of her father near Hebron, Washington county, by a shock
> of lightning, MARTHA ELIZABETH, daughter of Isaac R. YOUNGBLOOD, aged
> 19 years 4 months 27 days...was converted to religion at Zoar Camp Meeting
> in October last and joined the Methodist Church. (long eulogy)

27 June 1843

> Another Rev. hero gone. Died at Woolwich (Me.) the 5th instant,
> MR. JOHN SHAW, in the 92d year of his age. He served during the whole
> Rev. War.

> Still another. Died at Pittsburg on Tuesday morning at 7 o'clock,
> MR. PETER BROWN, aged 105 years. Mr. Brown was a native of France. He came
> to this country with General LaFayette, and fought in several battles
> during the Rev. War.

> From the Vicksburg Sentinel of June 12. A great man fallen! The people's
> champion dead!! DR. JAMES HAGAN is NO MORE!!! It becomes our painful duty
> to announce the cold blooded Assassination of the proprietor of this
> Journal yesterday afternoon at 3 o'clock P.M. at the hands of D.W. Adams,
> son of Judge George Adams, of Jackson...

> A rare old man. Died in this city on Friday evening the 2d inst. JOHN CARY,
> in the 114th year of his age. Was born of African parents, in Westmoreland
> county, Virginia in August 1729; accompanied Gen. Washington as his personal
> servant in the olf French war, and was with him in the battlefield on the
> Monongahela in July 1755...member of the Baptist Church (National
> Intelligencer, June 15th)

> Departed this life on Thursday the 22d instant in this City, MR. GEORGE
> STEELE, in the 31st year of his age. Was a native of Hartford, Conn. but
> removed in his infancy with his parents to Georgia; served apprenticeship
> to the printing business in Milledgeville. (long eulogy)

4 July 1843

> Died in this city Tuesday 27th ult., MARY ANN, infant daughter of
> Mr. and Mrs. Wm. BARNES, aged 4 months.

> Died at Troupville, Lowndes county, on Wednesday the 22d ult., ELIZABETH,
> wife of Morgan G. SWAIN, aged 33 years, after an illness of five weeks; a
> member of the Baptist Church for the last 13 years; left a disconsolate
> husband and five helpless children.

> Proclamation by Gov. Charles J. McDonald offering $150 reward for the
> apprehension of Anderson Morris for murder committed upon the body of
> the son of William BRIDGES in Meriwether county on 3d day of April last.

11 July 1843

> Sudden death. The Bay State Democrat of Tuesday evening announces the
> death on Saturday morning of the Rev. DAVID DAMON, pastor of the Unitarian
> Society of West Cambridge...

25 July 1843

Died in Sumter county on the 12th inst. in the 75th year of his age, JOSEPH DOUGLAS; a native of Mecklenburg county, North Carolina but came from South Carolina to Culloden, in Monroe county, where he resided for several years. (short eulogy)

Died in this place on Tuesday the 11th inst., MRS. REBECCA HILLYER, aged 57 years, after an illness of about three months...member of the Baptist Church; left an aged mother and children. (Athens Banner)

8 Aug 1843

HON. JOHN HOLMES died at Portland, Maine on Friday afternoon last after an illness of several months. He had formerly been US Senator from that State...

Departed this life on the 29th ult. at the summer residence of his father near Augusta, MR. OSWELL EVE CARMICHAEL, in the 33d year of his age... (long eulogy)

Died in Lee county, Ga. on the 29th ult., MRS. ALICE McCOMB, consort of Mr. Samuel McComb, recently of this city, now of Lee county, but formerly a resident of Charlotte, North Carolina. (short eulogy)

Died in this City on Saturday evening 29th ult. in her 16th year, MISS REBECCA ANN LAMAR, daughter and only child of Gen. Mirabeau B. Lamar, late President of the Republic of Texas. (long eulogy) (Macon Messenger)

22 Aug 1843

Died in LaGrange 15th inst., PLEASANT WIMBERLY, son of the Rev. C.W. KEY, aged 21 months 6 days.

Proclamation by Gov. Charles J. McDonald offering $150 reward for the apprehension of person or persons who committed murder upon the body of SEABORN J. POLLARD in Greene county on the night of the 18th ultimo...

29 Aug 1843

Died in Milledgeville on the 23d inst. MRS. SARAH P. WADE, in the 74th year of her age - a native of Virginia but for the greater part of her life a resident of this state; member of the Baptist Church. (short eulogy)

5 Sep 1843

Died in this city on the 27th ult., ROBERT WILBURN, in the 63d year of his age; a Virginian by birth and a Georgian by adoption; an exemplary member of the Baptist Church; left a wife and daughter.

12 Sep 1843

Died at his residence in Dooly county on the 3d inst., ARTHUR A. MORGAN, Esq., late Judge of the Southern Circuit. His disease was congestive measles; a native Georgian, in his 42d year. (short eulogy)

Proclamation by Gov. Charles J. McDonald offering $150 reward for the
apprehension of Abner Sermon for murder committed upon the body of
ALLEN WEST in Lowndes county 4 Oct 1839...

26 Sep 1843
Departed this life, of Typhus Fever, on Friday 22d inst. at 11 o'clock
in Sandersville, at the residence of Dr. J.P. Welch, his relative,
THOMAS HUDSON WHITAKER in the 16th year of his age; leaves mother, sister,
two brothers - (short eulogy)

3 Oct 1843
Died at his residence in Baldwin county on the 24th Sep 1843,
MR. BENJAMIN HALL, aged 71 years. The deceased was born in Chatham county,
North Carolina, from whence he removed at the age of 7 or 8 years to
Warren county in this State, where he resided 24 years - thence he removed
to Hancock county, where he remained 22 years, and from thence to Baldwin
county...by occupation a farmer; member of the Baptist Church for 40 years.
(short eulogy)

A most brutal murder was committed near Knoxville, Tenn. on the 5th instant
on the person of JOHN SUTTON, a soldier of the Revolution, aged 95 years,
for the sake of obtaining $33, the pension money which the old man had
drawn that day.

Headed Agent's Office, Fort Gibson, C.N., August 9, 1843. ISAAC BUSHBYHEAD
and ELIJAH HICKS were both murdered, and David Vann, treasurer of the
nation, dangerously wounded...

Death by lightning. The house of Mr. Albert E. Cox, in this county, was
struck by lightning about 3 o'clock last Sunday morning. Mr. Cox, who was
in bed, on recovering from the stunning effect of the shock, found his
wife MRS. NANCY E. COX dead by his side...their child who was in the same
bed was uninjured... (Washington News)

10 Oct 1843
Died in Monticello on Saturday the 16th ult. of a protracted illness,
MR. WILLIAM McKENDREE BRODDUS, aged 35 years, late a member of the firm
of Smith & Broddus, merchants of Hillsboro, T.J. Smith & Co., of Monticello.
(short eulogy)

17 Oct 1843
Melancholy accident. MR. DANIEL PRATT of this county came to an untimely
end on Friday night last. He had walked out after supper to go to a
neighbor's; while on the way, he had occasion to handle a pistol he had
in his belt or waistband - and when in the act of returning it to its place,
it exploded, the ball entering his hip where it lodged. He was able to
reach the house he was going to and explain the circumstances of the
accident; but lived only a few hours after. (Macon Telegraph, 10th inst.)

The Van Buren (Arkansas) Intelligencer of the 9th inst. has received the painful intelligence of the death of DAVID VANN, treasurer of the Cherokee nation. He died at his residence at the Saline on the 2d inst. of the wounds inflicted upon him by a lawless mob, on the 8th ult.

Died at his residence in Washington county, of typhus fever on Tuesday the 3d inst., MR. ABEL HODGE, in the 70th year of his age; an exemplary member of the Methodist Episcopal Church for the last 17 years; left an aged widow and several children.

Died in Wilkinson county on Sunday morning the 15th inst., of fever, MR. GEORGE W. JOHNSON, about 35 years of age.

Died in Hillsboro on the evening of the 10th inst., MRS. ELIZA FRANCES KEENE, wife of Dr. B.F. Keene and eldest daughter of Cuthbert Reese, Esq., aged 19 years 3 months.

Died in Jasper county 1st inst., SAMUEL HOWARD, in the 63d year of his age, and NANCY HOWARD his wife, aged 61 years. They were attacked about the same time and died within nine hours of each other. (eulogy)

24 Oct 1843
    Died at his residence in this county on Monday the 16th inst.,
HORATIO N. BARKSDALE, aged 42 years. He bore an illness of eight weeks with remarkable patience; leaves a wife and children.

Died in this city on the 12th inst. of Typhus Fever, MRS. ELIZABETH Y. BEACH, consort of Mr. Isaac C. Beach, in the 33d year of her age, leaving an affectionate husband and infant daughter; native of Morris County, New Jersey, where her parents now reside, but for the last two years had been a resident of this city. (long (eulogy)

THOMAS D. RICE, the Commercial Editor of the Georgian, is no more. Confined for about a week to his house with an attack of fever...but yesterday afternoon it assumed an unfavorable change, and our friend sunk under it between twelve and one o'clock last night. (Savannah Georgian)

31 Oct 1843
    Died at his residence near Darien, Ga. on the evening of the 18th inst.,
MAJ. JOHN H.N. McINTOSH, in the 60th year of his age. A native of Georgia and a son of the late Maj. Gen. John McIntosh - a soldier of the Revolution and the late war of 1812; entered the Army at an early age and served during the late war with England, on our Northern frontier, and in Canada; also attached to the Southern and Western Army- and served with Gen. Jackson throughout his Indian Campaigns; resigned his Majority in the Army in 1820 and was appointed Collector of Custons of this district, which office he resigned, after having held it for a number of years; leaves a large and afflicted family.

14 Nov 1843
    Died at her residence in Jasper county, MRS. SOPHIA CURRY, wife of
Thompson Curry, aged 28 years; had been afflicted with pulmonary consumption. (short eulogy)

83

Departed this life on Thursday morning the 2d inst., MILLER J. HOOD,
Junior Publisher of the "Pioneer." Was born 5th of April 1821. About four
weeks since he was seized with the prevailing influenza...in his death
his father's family have received a severe and heavy stroke... (long eulogy)
(Cassville Pioneer, 3d inst.)

28 Nov 1843

Died in this City on Wednesday last the 22d Nov. after a short illness,
MR. ROBERT CHRISTIAN, aged about 46 years, assistant Postmaster at this
place, and formerly for a number of years the Foreman of the "Georgia
Journal" office. A native of Lynchburg, Virginia (or its vicinity) but a
resident of this place for the last 23 years. (Richmond Enquirer and Lynchburg
Virginian will please copy)

A bloody tragedy. A letter received in this city from Sparta, Hancock
county, says - "Yesterday a negro belonging to Jos. R. SARSNETT was hung in
this place for an attempt to murder his master; and yesterday, or rather
the evening previous, John Lawson killed OBEDIAH CULVER and ENOCH JACKSON...
Jackson, we understand, married Lawson's sister, and out of this marriage
grew the difficulty between them." (Sav. Georgian, 20th inst.)

5 Dec 1843

Departed this life on Monday 23d of October, MRS. SARAH BRANTLY, aged
54 years; was when quite young united in marriage to Mr. John Shockley -
also a member of the Baptist Church, with whom she lived until they reared
a family of children, when it pleased the Lord to remove her companion to
his rest. Sometime after the death of her first husband, she was married to
Mr. Benjamin Brantly, of Jones county, also a member of the Baptist Church.
During the last four years of her life has been severely afflicted.
(long eulogy)

Sudden death. DR. DADE, the brother of the gallant major who fell in
Florida, died very suddenly on the 16th inst. in King George County, Va....
he seated himself in his carriage and was observed to check his horse so
violently as to throw him down. The doctor then fell forward to the ground
and never spoke again.

12 Dec 1843

MR. EDWIN WHITAKER, of this city, departed this life on the morning of the
7th inst., in the 48th year of his age1 had long been a member of the
Methodist E. Church. (eulogy)

19 Dec 1843

Died at his residence in Butts county, Ga. on the 8th inst. of Bilious
Pleurisy, Doctor JOHN SAUNDERS, in the 62d year of his age. He was a native
of Virginia (Isle of Wight county); left a widow and two children.
(short eulogy) (Richmond Enquirer will please publish)

26 Dec 1843

Departed this life on the 17th ult. at his residence in Wilkinson county,
Elder JOHN HUGHES, who had been some 35 years a member of the Baptist Church,
and for about 14 years a pious Minister of the Gospel...his disease was
inflammation of the lungs.

Died of child bed fever in Baker county on the 11th of Dec 1843,
MRS. MARY CARTER HOLMES, consort of Thos. J. Holmes, aged 31 years 5 months
14 days; for four years a pious member of the Methodist Church; she had
lived to see five of her children buried; only one remaining child surives.

9 Jan 1844

Died in this place on the 21st ult., MR. JOHN L. RAGSDALE, a native of
Brunsick or Mecklenburg county, Virginia, but for many years past a
resident of this city. His remains were interred with military honors
by the "Metropolitan Greys" of which corps he was a member.
(Virginia papers will please publish)

16 Jan 1844

Died at the residence of her father in Wilkinson county on Tuesday the
5th of December, AMANDA CAROLINE, eldest daughter of Col. Green B. BURNEY,
aged 14 years. Had lived a member of the Methodist E. Church only about
3 months - embraced religion at the last Camp Meeting in Wilkinson county.
(long eulogy)

23 Jan 1844

Died at his residence in Jasper county on the 12th December, MR. JOHN B.
GILLSTRAP, aged about 35 years; has left a disocnsolate mother. (eulogy)

Murder. MR. EDWARD W. COLLIER was stabbed to death yesterday morning
at about 3 or 4 o'clock, near the Rail Road depot, and a few minutes after
the arrival of the cars from Madison. The deceased kept the Richmond
Hotel and the murderer was attached to the United States Hotel. The quarrel
between them originated no doubt about the accomodations afforded to
passengers... (Augusta Constitutionalist, Jan. 6)

6 Feb 1844

Died near Blountsville, Jones county, on the 25th ult., MRS. ASENETH S. MILLER,
in the 64th year of her age, widow of the late John J. Miller. Was one
of the first settlers of Jones county, and for many years a worthy member
of the Baptist Church.

Death of Gov. Kavanagh. From the Eastern Argus of Tuesday - Died at his
residence in New Castle, HON. EDWARD KAVANAGH, on Sunday evening 21st at
10 o'clock P.M., aged 48 years. Was born at New Castle 27 Apr 1795 -
consequently he was 48 years old on 27th day of April last.

Announcement of the death of HON. WILLIAM GASTON, one of the Judges of the
Supreme Court of North Carolina. He expired very suddenly (at the
residence of Mrs. Taylor, in this city) last evening about eight o'clock.
(Raleigh Standard)

13 Feb 1844

Died at his residence in Hawkinsville on the 27th Jan last of Rheumatism
and Erysipelas, JOHN RAWLS. The deceased removed from the county of Bulloch
to the county of Pulaski in 1816 and continued to reside there until his
death. Was member of the State Legislature and President of the Bank of Hawkinsville. His name was placed upon an electoral ticket of President and
Vice-President of the United States.

27 Feb 1844

Died in this city on the evening of the 21st instant of Quinzy,
MISS SARAH, daughter of Samuel and Rebecca BREEDLOVE, in the 19th year
of her age. (long eulogy)

Departed this life on the 13th February in the county of Putnam,
MRS. NISEY SINGLETON, wife of Leroy Singleton, in the 35th year of
her age; leaves husband and five children. (short eulogy)

26 Mar 1844

Correspondence of the Columbia Chronicle. Headed Edgefield C.H.
March 16, 1844. Daniel Deas, alias Graham, alias Rogers, was today
sentenced to be hung on Friday the 10th of May next by Judge Richardson.
He was found guilty of the murder of WM. BAREFOOT (his step-father)
who had brought himp up and made him an accomplice in committing criminal
offences... (long article)

9 Apr 1844

Died in Meriwether county on Monday evening the 26th of March, of
dropsy of the chest, MRS. MARY TUCKER, in the 76ht year of her age.
She was a native of Virginia, and emigrated to Georgia upwards of
48 years past. She united herself to the Methodist Episcopal Church
nearly forty years ago...Her sleeping remains lie entombed at the family
burying-ground at the former residence of Mr. James Crowder.

16 Apr 1844

The HON. HEMAN A. MOORE, representative in Congress from Ohio, died
at Columbus on the 3d inst...

Shocking murder. The Natchez (Miss.) Courier of the 28th ult. gives
particulars of the murder of a MISS DEMOSS, who was killed about the
15th near Minden, Claiborne parish, La.

23 Apr 1844

Died in this city on Monday the 15th inst. after four weeks' severe
suffering with Hydrocephalus, KOSCIUSKO, only son of Mr. Charles E.
and Mrs. Mary Ann RYAN, aged 21 months (short eulogy)

30 Apr 1844

Died in this county on the 16th inst., FRANCIS DELAUNAY, Esq., Attorney
at Law, aged 41 years, a native of Virginia. He has left a widow and
seven children.

JUDGE HENRY BALDWIN, one of the Judges of the Supreme Court of the
United States, died in Philadelphia at 9 o'clock last night, of
paralysis, in the 65th year of his age. He was appointed a judge of
the Supreme Court by General Jackson 14 or 15 years ago. He resided at
Pittsburg, Pa. at the time of his appointment.

We learn from the Providence Journal that the trial of John and William
Gordon for the murder of MR. SPRAGUE was brought to a close on Wed. evening...

7 May 1844

Died at his residence in Paulding county on the 18th ult., JOHN BARTON, after
having suffered a number of years with palsy; an orderly member of
the Baptist Church, and at the time of his death in the 77th year of
his age.

14 May 1844

Departed this life in Baldwin county on the 6th inst., MR. WILLIAM
ANDERSON, in the 72d year of his age, a native of Virginia but for
the last 38 years a resident of this State; esteemed soldier of the
Revolution which "tried men's souls"; member of the Baptist Church.

Died in this city on the 3d inst. of protracted consumption, MR. BENJAMIN S.W.
SELBY, in the 38th year of his age, a Printer by profession.
(short eulogy)

21 May 1844

A corrected obituary on MR. WILLIAM ANDERSON. He departed this life
in Baldin county on the 6th inst., in the 82nd year of his age; a
native of Virginia but for the last 38 years a resident of this county;
a Rev. patriot and member of the Baptist Church.

28 May 1844

Departed this life in Jones county on the 4th day of April last,
MRS. SUSAN H. JUHAN, wife of Mr. Isaac B. Juhan of that county, in the
35th year of her age; for 16 years an exemplary member of the Baptist
Church; leaves a bereaved husband and children. (eulogy)

Died in this city on the 17th inst. of Erysipelas, MRS. MARY BUFFINGTON,
wife of Saml. Buffington, Sr., Esq., in the 57th year of her age. She
was a native of Washington county; member of the Baptist Church.

Died on Friday the 24th inst. in the 67th year of his age at his
residence in Midway, near Milledgeville, THOMAS FOARD, a native of
Virginia but for more than 40 years a citizen of this State; member of
the Methodist Epis. Church.

Died in Macon on Saturday 18th inst., MRS. MARY F. CLEVELAND, relict of
Hon. Jesse F. Cleveland and daughter of Maj. James Smith, aged about 28.

Headed Eatonton, April 13th, 1844. Tribute of Respect by members of
Rising Star Lodge on the death of Bro. IRBY HUDSON, who departed this life
yesterday.

18 June 1844

Murder. A most daring and atrocious murder was committed during Tuesday
night last, on the body of MR. GEORGE LYON, watch maker and jeweller,
residing on the west side of East Bay, a few doors south of Queen street...
(Charleston Courier, 13th inst.)

25 June 1844
   Suicide. A Jury of Inquest was impaneled on Wed. night last on the
   body of THOMAS THURSTAND, who has been in Jail in this city, awaiting
   his trial for an alleged forgery on the Planters & Mechanic Bank. The
   Jury returned a verdict that the deceased came to his death by taking
   poison... (Charleston Courier)

   Died on Sat. 22d inst. at his residence in this city, WILLIAM MEDFORD,
   aged 67 years. He left several children and numerous relatives to
   mourn their loss.

9 July 1844
   Died near Milledgeville May 24th, 1844, THOMAS FOARD, in the 67th year
   of his age. Born in Virginia but removed to Georgia in early life. Was
   converted and joined the church about forty years ago in Hancock county.
   (eulogy)

   Died at his residence, in the Asylum, near this place, on the 11th ult.,
   WILLIAM B. MOORE, aged 32. Had occupied the station of Steward in the
   Lunatic Asylum from the time of its organization. Leaves a widow and
   several young children.

   Died in Marietta on Sat. night the 15th ult. at 10½ o'clock,
   MISS JULIA STILES, daughter of Maj. Wm. Y. and Mrs. Susan HANSELL, aged
   17 years 3 months...in 1839 made public profession of religion and
   attached herself to the Presbyterian Church in Milledgeville, where her
   father then resided... (long eulogy)

16 July 1844
   Died this day (the 4th of July) between 12 and 1 o'clock P.M., in
   Eatonton, after a lingering illness of some 10 or 11 months, originating
   from hemorrhage of the lungs, MAJ. ALBERT JONES, of this place, about
   40 years of age... (long eulogy)

   Died at his residence in Jasper county on Sunday night the 23d ult., the
   REV. DAVID L. ADAMS, in the 46th year of his age, leaving a widow and a
   large family of children...was born in Hancock county, and has for many
   years resided in Jasper county; member of the Baptist Church. (eulogy)

   Died at the residence of her son John Robinson, Esq. in Jasper county
   on the 29th day of June, MRS. LYDIA ROBINSON, in her 80th year; member
   of the Baptist Church about 50 years. (long eulogy)

   Died in Americus, Ga. on the 4th inst. of Pertussis, MYLES FREDERICK,
   infant son of Dr. A.B. and Mrs. R.H. GREENE, aged 2 months 14 days.

30 July 1844
   Sudden death. On the 11th inst. DR. B.L. FRANKLIN, aged about 26 years,
   and formerly a resident of our city, was instantaneously killed at a
   mining establishment in Cherokee county, Ga. by the machinery employed
   in the works. (Macon Messenger)

6 Aug 1844

Departed this life on the 31st July at the residence of his brother in Jasper county, JOHN DANIEL, aged about 32 years...During the absence from home of his brother and family, the deceased having retired to his room, put an end to his existence by shooting himself, having applied the instrument of death to his right temple...

Departed this life in this city on Friday the 2d inst., PAULINA, infant child of Sydney and Ann SWEETZER, aged 9 months 13 days.

Died in Newton county, Georgia on Sat. the 13th of July 1844, after an illness of eight days from Congestive Fever, MRS. MARIA JOUETT WHATLEY, consort of B.O.W. Whatley, Esq., of this county. Was the daughter of Larkin and Henrietta Johnson. Was born in Oglethorpe county, Ga. on 8 Apr 1809; leaves husband, three children, and aged mother, and a brother and a sister. (eulogy) (Signed J.D.J. - Newton county, July 29th, 1844) (The Southern Recorder will please copy)

20 Aug 1844

Died at Scottsboro on the 25th ultimo, MRS. MARY CULLENS, consort of Wiley W. Cullens, Esq.; member of Methodist E. Church... (long eulogy)

Died in this city on the 17th inst., MRS. MATILDA MEDFORD, in the 58th year of her age, and for the last 20 years a worthy member of the Baptist Church.

27 Aug 1844

Death of MR. JAMES WILLINGHAM was occasioned by the falling in of the front of a house which had been blown down in part by powder. Was a foreman in our office... (Telegraph, 20th inst.)

3 Sep 1844

That venerable and devoted servant of Christ, REV. WILSON CONNER, literally fell at his post on the 5th Sabbath in June last (not on Wed. as heretofore stated by mistake). The writer believes he was a native of North Carolina... (long eulogy)

24 Sep 1844

Died very suddenly on Sat. the 21st inst., MARY WOOLWORTH, eldest though yet infant daughter of Dr. Geo. D. CASE, of this city (eulogy).

15 Oct 1844

Departed this life at their residence in this county on the 27th Sept., MRS. CATHARINE: consort of Major William F. SCOTT. Her last illness was billious fever, which closed her earthly existence after a continuance of 24 days; member of the Baptist Church in this city about ten years; leaves husband. (eulogy)

Departed this life on the 10th ult. at his residence near Macon, LUKE ROSS, Esq., in the 69th year of his age; was born in NC where he resided until about the year 1799, when he removed to this State.

22 Oct 1844
    Died on Sunday evening the 13th inst. in this city, DONALD M. McDONALD,
    Clerk of the Superior Court of Baldwin county.

5 Nov 1844
    Fatal accident. MR. JAMES C. COOK was killed at his own door by a
    frightened horse, attached to a buggy, in which he was just about to
    enter. It is supposed his hands became intangled in the reins, and in
    that situation he was dashed against a tree; was one of the oldest
    citizens of Columbus. (Columbus Times, 23d ult)

    Died in Galveston, Texas on the 31st of July last, MISS MARY ANN SUSAN
    McDONALD, in the 24th year of her age.

    Died also in Galveston on the 23d of September, MRS. ELIZA CARTER FRANKLIN,
    in the 31st year of her age.

    Died in Scottsboro, Georgia on the 15th day of October, MRS. MARY ANN DAVIS,
    in the 26th year of her age. (eulogy to this and the two previous deaths)

    Died at Scottsboro on the 26th inst., ANNA GEORGIA, infant danughter of
    W.W. CULLENS, aged 3 months 1 day (eulogy).

    Died in Monroe County, Georgia on the 7th inst. of remittant fever, after
    an illness of 18 days, JAMES TURNER, Esq., in the 44th year of his age...
    about 1828 attached himself to the M.E. Church; was member of the
    Legislature of Georgia and a Justice of the Peace for many years...leaves wife,
    eight children, an aged father and mother, several brothers and sisters.
    (long eulogy).

    Died at their residence in Pineville, Marion county, Georgia, of bilious
    fever, DANIEL M. HALL and his two eldest sons. Daniel M. Hall died on
    the 13th day of Sep 1844, aged 48 years 2 months 2 days, after an illness
    of eight days; his eldest son JOHN W. HALL, taken ill about the same time,
    died on the 14th day of the same month, aged 23 years 11 months 23 days,
    after an illness of ten days; ISAAC HALL, second son of Daniel M., taken
    about the same time, died the 17th day of the same month, after an illness
    of 13 days, aged 22 years 27 days. Daniel M. Hall was well known as a
    citizen of Georgia, especially in the county of Wilkinson, the place of
    his former residence, and in our State Legislature at different times; a
    member of the Baptist Church of the Primitive order for some 14 or 15 years;
    leaves wife, six surviving children, father (eulogy).

    Departed this life on Sat. the 19th Oct 1844 in Monticello, Georgia,
    LUCY ANN, daughter of Col. John A. and Arena DILLARD, aged 2 years
    7 months 7 days. (short eulogy)

12 Nov 1844
    Terrible steamboat disaster. Explosion of the Lucy Warner. 60 to 80
    people killed and wounded. Killed and missing: Gen. J.W. PEGRAM, of
    Richmond, Va; SAMUEL M. BROWN, Post Office Agent of Lexington, Ky;
    J.R. CORMICK, of Virginia; CHARLES DONNE, of Louisville; PHILLIP WALLIS,
    formerly of Baltimore; REBECCA, daughter of A.J. FOSTER, of Greenville, Va;
    JAMES VANDERBERG, of Louisville; MR. HUGHS, formerly of Lexington, Ky;
    MR. MUTTOCK, of New Albany, engineer of the steamboat Mazeppa; NICHOLAS FORD,
    formerly of this city; DAVID VANN, the Captain; MOSES KIRBY, Pilot...

19 Nov 1844

The Brandon (Mass) Advocate says that H.G. RUNNELS, formerly Governor of the State, has met a violent death. Report says he was assassinated by a band of lawless rascalls, who waylaid and shot him.

From the Columbus Enquirer. Painful accident. A most melancholy accident happened in this city on Sat. last by which a sprightly and intelligent lad, aged 12 years, a son of Judge STURGIS, lost his life...

Died at Carnesville on Sat. morning 26th ult. at 2 o'clock, CLARISSA LOUISA, youngest daughter of Dr. Henry and Martha M. FREEMAN, aged 7 years 24 days.

Died in Jones county on the 29th of October, in the 80th year of his age, BENJAMIN BRANTLEY, Esq. - a native of North Carolina but removed to this State in 1800 and settled in Hancock county, where he resided until 1835, when he removed to Jones county; member of the Baptist Church.

3 Dec 1844

Died on the 28th Oct. at her residence in Jasper county, MRS. ELIZABETH DARDEN, in the 66th year of her age.

The Chattanooga Gazette of the 16th inst. announces the death at Pileville, Tenn. of the notorious JOHN A. MURRELL whose name as a "land pirate" figured so frequently in the press some years since, and who was recently discharged from the penitentiary. He died of consumption.

17 Dec 1844

Died in Bloomfield (Maine) on the 23d ult., MRS. MARY, wife of Gen. Joseph LOCKE, aged 62 years. The deceased was the mother of the Senior Editor of this paper, who is now absent in Europe. She died suddenly from a disease of the heart. (Sav. Republican)

21 Jan 1845

Hon. W.W. SOUTHGATE, of Kentucky, formerly a member of Congress, died at Covington a few days since.

Died at the Flinthill Camp-ground on the evening of the 24th ult., in Gwinnett county, Ga., MR. JOHN A., eldest son of Mr. Coalman B. MONDAY, formerly of Greenville District, South Carolina, aged 25 years 19 days. The deceased came to his death by being shot by one of the company discharging a gun that was said not to be loaded... (short eulogy)

11 Feb 1845

Murder. ROBERT P. BALDWIN was found dead, says the Macon Messenger, on Friday morning the 17th ult. in Monroe county, about two and a half miles from Forsyth. We learn that he had been to Forsyth the evening previous, and was murdered by being beaten on the head, on his return home, by some person or persons yet unknown...

18 Feb 1845

> MRS. ELIZA SARAH SCHLEY, consort of the Hon. William Schley, departed this life on the night of the 11th instant, after enduring the sufferings occasioned by cancer for nearly two years; member of the Methodist Episcopal Church (eulogy)

25 Feb 1845

> Departed this life at Greenhill, Washington county, the residence of her father, on Tuesday the 11th instant at 8 minutes past 11 o'clock AM, MRS. ANNA W. FIELD, wife of Mr. Samuel Field, and only daughter of Mr. Isham H. and Mrs. Patience Saffold, after an illness of four or five days...her infant son who had passed but a few hours before her... (long eulogy)

4 Mar 1845

> Died in Tallahassee, Florida on Wed. the 12th ult., MRS. MARY MYERS, in the 55th year of her age; member of Methodist Episcopal Church and the mother of Rev. E.H. Myers, of the Georgia Conference.

18 Mar 1845

> Died in this city on the 8th inst., AMY VIRGINIA, daughter of Col. A.W. and Mrs. Susan K. REDDING, aged 1 year 2 months.

> Died on the 13th inst., PETER, infant son of Mr. Moses and Mrs. Sarah CHARAKER, aged about 3 months.

> "In the midst of life we are in death." The Baltimore Sun records an instance of the truth of the above caption on the sudden decease of a young lady of Washington city. The following notices appear side by side --- Married at Washington city on Thursday last, 13th inst., by the Rev. Norval Wilson, Mr. James Westcott to Miss Harriet Ann Calvert, both of that city. -- Died at Washington city on Wed., 19th inst., Mrs. Harriet Ann, wife of Mr. James Westcott, in the 20th year of her age...

8 Apr 1845

> Died in this city on the 3d inst., CLAIBOURN COOPER, infant son of Col. N.C. and Mrs. Mary A. BARNETT, aged 16 months 17 days.

> REV. WILLIAM T. BRANTLY, D.D., late Pastor of the First Baptist Church in this city and late President of the College of Charleston, departed this life on Friday last in Augusta, whither he had removed in the hope of alleviating his suffering condition. Dr. Brantly was one of the earliest students of the South Carolina College, having graduated with distinction in that institution in 1808... (Charleston Courier, 31st ult)

> Suicide. The Savannah Republican of the 29th ult. reports the termination of the life of a young and promising clergyman of the Episcopal Church of this place - the REV. JAMES JACKSON, late of the Diocese of Massachusetts...

22 Apr 1845

Desperate affray. A most bloody affray occurred in Hernando, Miss. between several men, some eight or ten days since...occurred between T.J. Matlock, Esq., and his brother and overseer on one side, and a Mr. Forrest on the other. It seems the Matlocks had a dispute with another person, when young Mr. Forrest made some interfering remarks...induced one of the Matlocks to raise a stick to strike Forrest, who immediately drew a revolving pistol...young Mr. Forrest received a slight pistol wound in his arm. The most melancholy part of the bloody affray was the death of old MR. FORREST, father of the other, who stood some yards off, he was deliberately shot down by Mr. Matlock's overseer, without the least provocation. (Memphis Eagle, 21st ult)

20 May 1845

Died in this city, of Scarlet fever complicated with Croup, WILLIAM JOHN, son of Dr. Thomas F. and Mrs. Adeline E. GREEN, in the 7th year of his age. (long eulogy)

3 June 1845

The Hon. JOHN CAMPBELL, for many years a member of Congress from the Peedee District (SC), died at his residence in Marlborough District on Monday week of hemorrhage of the lungs.

10 June 1845

Fatal accident on the Central R.R. On Monday 2d inst., as the passenger train was passing down from Gordon, about one mile below, they ran over MR. JESSE COLLIER, aged 68 years, killing him instantly.

24 June 1845

Departed this life on the morning of the 14th inst., after a very brief illness, at his residence in this city, COL. JOHN LAMAR, in the 34th year of his age...was born in the neighboring county of Jones, and educated at Franklin College in this State; entered Cambridge Law Scool in Boston; member of the Legislature from this county in 1842 and one of the delegates to the National Convention at Baltimore which nominated Mr. Polk; funeral services took place at his late residence on Sunday morning, and his mortal remains were interred at Rose Hill Cemetery (long eulogy) (Macon Telegraph, 18th inst)

Died in Columbus on Sunday morning the 8th inst. of Consumption, MISS ANTOINETTE RUSSEAU, in the 21st year of her age.

Died at his residence in Jasper county on the 30th May, MR. JAMES C. FLEMISTER, aged about 49 years; attached himself to the M.E. Church about 1838; leaves a wife and children (short eulogy)

1 Jul 1845

Died near this place on Wed. the 25th ult., THOMAS HOLMES KENAN, second son of M.J. and C.A. Kenan, aged 7 years 2 months. And on Friday the 27th, ELIZA HOUSTOUN KENAN, their second daughter, aged 5 years 3 months 21 days.

Died in Eatonton on the morning of the 23d ult., in the 23d year of
his age, DR. ALONZO J. TRIPPE. His murder was committed by a young
man by the name of A.B. Hoxey, son of Dr. Hoxey of Columbus. The murder
was committed by stabbing, which caused death instantaneously.

8 Jul 1845

Died on the 15th ult. after a short illness of pain in the breast, at
the residence of Wetham Bowen, Esq., at Bowensville, Irwin county,
MR. FRANCIS G. RIODEN, formerly of Lee county, aged about 22 years.

15 Jul 1845

General JOHN B. DAWSON, member of the last Congress, died at St. Francisville,
La. on the 26th ult., in the prime of life...

Coroner's report - from the Constitutionalist. Died at his mother's
residence in this city on the seventh day of July instant, MR. JOSIAH W.
THOMPSON. The deceased was shot on the 26th day of June last, with a gun
loaded with buck shot, and languished until the morning of the 7th day
of July, and died in consequence of the wounds. Jury returned a verdict
that the deceased came to his death at the hands of E.A. Dye -
Justifiable Homicide.

22 Jul 1845

Headed Company Room, Metropolitan Greys, July 16th, 1845. Tribute of
Respect on the death of JAMES F.M. REDDING, a member who died on Monday
the 14th instant...

Another patriot of the Revolution dead. Died at Greenwich, Conn. on the
8th day of June, of small pox, NOAH LOCKWOOD, aged 91 years. He was one
of the first to enter the army at the first outbreak of the Revolution,
and was an active participant in the struglles at Lexington, Bunker Hill,
Concord, and Yorktown.

Died in this city on the 19th inst. of Scarlet Fever, OWEN HOLMES,
youngest son of M.J. and Catherine A. KENAN, in the 5th year of his age.

Died of Typhus Fever, after a short illness, at the residence of Maj. Allen
Little in Baldwin county, on the 17th inst., ELIZABETH ANN LITTLE, only
daughter of Major Allen and Margaret Ellen Little - aged 13 years 7 months
4 days. The deceased was a pupil of the Female School of this city.
(long eulogy)

29 Jul 1845

Died in this city on the 18th inst. of Consumption, MRS. MARY STEPHENS,
aged 72 years. Was born in the vicinity of Linnox, Miss. - at the age of
16 she attached herself to the Presbyterian Church - was subsequently
married, and in 1808 removed with her family to Virginia; there being no
Presbyterian Church in her neighborhood, she became a member of the
Methodist Church... (short eulogy)

5 Aug 1845

Died in this city on the 28th ult. after a protracted and painful illness, MRS. SARAH JOHNSON, wife of Thomas A. Johnson, in the 24th year of her age. For three years preceding her death, she was an orderly and respected member of the Methodist Church.

Died in Meriwether county on Wed. the 11th ult., of scarlet fever, MARY ELIZABETH, youngest daughter of Mr. B.F. and Mrs. A.B. DENSE, aged 4 years 4 months 20 days; and on Sunday the 29th, CHARLES FREDERICK, their youngest son, aged 3 years 3 months.

Headed Company Room, Metropolitan Greys, July 23, 1845. Tribute of Respect on the death of second sergeant JAMES D. ALLANON who departed life on the 22d inst.

26 Aug 1845

Died in this city on Wed. morning the 7th inst. of Typhus Fever, at the house of his father Col. N.C. Barnett, WILLIAM J.M. BARNETT, the only son, aged 19 years 3 months - a member of the Sophomore Class of Oglethorpe University. (long eulogy)

Died on the 10th inst. at his residence in Russel County, Alabama, in the 73rd year of his age, HENRY DARNELL, for many years a well known citizen of this place. (long eulogy)

9 Sep 1845

Died in Twiggs county July 3d in the fourth year of his age, TOMLINSON, son of Sarah and Laborn BECKCOM, and also, on the July 5th, in the third year of her age, their little daughter, SARAH ANN SUSAN...little BENJAMIN, who died Aug. 10th, in the third year of his age - only son and only child of Susan and Hardin T. SMITH. (eulogy)

Died on the 19th ult. at her father's residence in Baldwin county, Ga., MRS. MARY ELIZABETH B., wife of Mr. Eliphalet CHANDLER, formerly of Goshen county, N. Hampshire, in the 17th year of her age, after a painful affliction of three weeks duration. (Papers in N.H. and Vermont copy)

Died in Chambers county, Ala. on the 26th of June 1845, MRS. FRANCES S. WHATLEY, consort of Wyatt H. Whatley, and second daughter of Larkin and Henrietta Johnson, of Newton county, Ga. Was born in Oglethorpe county, Ga. on 17 Mar 1813; united with the Methodist Episcopal Church (long eulogy)

Died at Tucker's Cabins on the 17th ult. of bilious fever, after an illness of eleven days, AUGUSTUS M. ADAMSON, Esq., Post Master of that place, in the 26th year of his age; was for several years an acceptable member of the Methodist Church.

Headed Rising Star Lodge, No. 4, Eatonton, Georgia, August 19, 1845. Announced that JOHN G. LUMSDEN died suddenly on the 13th inst. of an acute attack of Cholera Morbus.

16 Sep 1845
> Died in Jasper county on the 15th of July, MRS. EMILY HINES, in
> the 19th year of her age, leaving a disconsolate husband and two
> little children... (short eulogy)

23 Sep 1845
> Judge STORY, LL.D., one of the Jutsices of the US Supreme Court,
> and Dane Professor of Law in Harvard University, died on Wed. last...
> (N.Y. Morning News, 12th inst.)

14 Oct 1845
> Died of Scarlet fever at Midway on the 4th inst., EDWARD, son of the
> Hon. C.B. COLE, aged 5 years (long eulogy)
>
> Died in Jasper county on the 12th ult. after a protracted illness of
> twelve months, MATTHEW JONES, one of our Revolutionary soldiers, aged
> 85 years 10 days. Was born in Virginia; married in Virginia after the
> Revolution, and soon after moved to North Carolina, where he lived some
> years, then removed to Georgia, where he raised up a respectable
> family, but survived them all in life except one, the wife of John
> Faulkner, in whose house he lingered and died, and by whom he was
> kindly nursed during his last illness...His surviving daughter and
> grandchildren hope to meet him in a better world.

4 Nov 1845
> Departed this life at her residence in this county on the 17th ult.,
> in the 49th year of her age, MRS. ROWELL, wife of Major Richard Rowell...
> (eulogy)

25 Nov 1845
> Died at Midway on the 19th inst., CARLTON B., son of the Hon. C.B. COLE,
> aged about 2 years (short eulogy)
>
> Died in Monroe county, Ga. on Friday the 14th of Nov 1845, THOMAS W. MORRIS,
> aged 50 years.
>
> Died in Irwin county, at the residence of his father, on the 28th ult.,
> of Billious fever, WOODSON WILCOX, son of James L. and Abigail Wilcox,
> aged 9 years.

2 Dec 1845
> DR. JAMES H. PEYTON, Whig member of Congress from the Nashville District,
> Tennessee, died at his residence a few days since.

9 Dec 1845
> Another Rev. soldier gone! Departed this life in the town of Covington,
> Newton county, on Thursday the 20th day of November, FRANCIS FARRAR, in
> the 82d year of his age. The deceased was a native of the county of
> Mecklenburg in Virginia, where he was born in April 1764. At the age of
> sixteen, he went in the service of his country...was in the battle at
> Guilford Court House...removed from Virginia to Georgia and settled in
> Augusta; united with the Baptist Church at Freeman's Creek in Clarke
> county. (eulogy)

16 Dec 1845

Died in Milledgeville on the 8th instant, of pulmonary affection, the representative of Baker county, JOHN HENTZ, Esq. (eulogy)

23 Dec 1845

Commodore JESSE D. ELLIOTT, a conspicuous Naval Officer, and Commandant of the Navy Yard at Philadelphia, died at his boarding house in that city a few days since. He was in the 62d year of his age.

30 Dec 1845

Died of Apoplexy on the 8th inst., at the age of 64 years, MOSES FORT, Esq. (short eulogy)

Died on the 21st December at the residence of her father Zach. Edmondson of Putnam county, his daughter ELIZABETH A. BROWN, consort of Oscar V. Brown of Bladwin county; leaves husband and infant son, a father, mother, two sisters and three brothers.

Died at Midway on Friday evening the 21st November after a short illness, HORACE VIRGIL, youngest son of Mrs. Sarah FISH, aged about 5 years. (eulogy)

Died on Monday Dec 6th at the house of her husband Mr. Thomas Lightfoot in Jones county, MINERVA OLIVE, fifth daughter of Nathaniel Turbiville, Esq. She expired at about 3 P.M. - aged 18 years.

13 Jan 1846

Died at the residence of Maj. M.D. Huson in this county, JOHN LITTLE, in the 74th year of his age. Was a native of Charlotte, Mecklenburg county, North Carolina, where he resided in the early part of his life many years, and then settled near Memphis, Tennessee, there he resided until about 1835, when he removed to Texas. From his advanced age and the exposures of a new country, he was there stricken with Palsy. He was thence brought by his relations in 1838 to this neighborhood. In his last years of suffering and weakness, he received the comforting attention and care of Mrs. Huson, his aged and only surviving sister, and of her family. (Charlotte papers will please copy)

Died at Macon on Wed. last, aged about 35 years, MRS. LOUISA M., wife of Edwin B. WEED, Esq.; member of the Presbyterian Church; leaves husband and children (long eulogy)

20 Jan 1846

Died in Hawkinsville January 7th, MR. JOSEPH M. COOPER, aged 26 years 28 days. He was for many years a consistent member of the Methodist Society. Has left a wife and child.

17 Feb 1846

Died in this city on the fifth inst. of Consumption, MRS. J.A. CUSHING, consort of I.T. Cushing, jr. Mrs. Cushing was in the 26th year of her age and left a husband and three children.

Died on the 26th ult. near Oxford, Ga., MRS. ANDREW, mother of
Rev. Bishop Andrew, in the 75th year of her age; a member of the
Methodist Episcopal Church nearly sixty years.

3 Mar 1846

Died in this city on Wed. the 11th ult., WILLIAMEINA, daughter of
Dr. John and Mrs. Catharine MITCHELL - aged 3 years 6 months; member of
M.E. Sabbath School. (long eulogy)

10 Mar 1846

Bloody tragedy. Inquest over the body of the late JOHN H. PLEASANTS.
An inquest was holden yesterday upon the body of John H. Pleasants,
deceased, before Coroner Robert T. Wicker...their verdict was that
Thomas Ritchie, Jr. was guilty of the murder of Pleasants in a mutual
combat had between them on the 25th instant, and that Peter Jefferson
Archer, Washington Greenhow, and William Scott were presen-, aiding and
abetting in said combat and in said murder. The Coroner has issued his
warrant to arrest said parties. (From the Richmond Times)

17 Mar 1846

The late Dr. Baber (AMBROSE BABER). Macon Telegraph announces the
sudden death of this gentleman. Was a native of Rockingham county,
Virginia, and after completing his education, emigrated in life to
this State, where he has resided ever since, with the exception of a
short absence in Europe. He served as Surgeon in the Army, under Gen.
Jackson in the Seminole campaign. Represented this county in both
branches of the legislature. In 1841 was appointed by Gen. Harrison
as minister to the Court of Turin in the Kingdom of Sardinia, in which
capacity he remained until the spring of 1844, when he returned to
this city and resumed the practice of his profession. Has left a wife
and three children of tender years to mourn their loss.

31 Mar 1846

Died in Washington City on the 18th inst., WALTER LUKE, infant son of
the Hon. Walter T. COLQUITT, of the U.S. Senate.

7 Apr 1846

Fatal rencontre. On Tuesday last a rencontre occurred in Macon between
FINLEY COLLINS and James M. Danielly. Several pistols were discharged.
The latter was slightly wounded in the arm, the former received a ball
in the chest which occasioned his death in a few hours.

14 Apr 1846

Died at his residence in this county on the 6th inst., EDWARD W. BUTLER,
in the 63d year of his age.

Died March 11th in Twiggs county, in the 31st year of his age, ROBERT
RICKS ARRINGTON, Was born in Nash county, North Carolina and when quite
young, his father Thomas Arrington immigrated to this county and soon
died leaving a widow and many children, of whom the subject of this notice
was the oldest, being then only 13 years old. In 1840 he lost the best
of mothers... (long eulogy)

Died in Marion, Twiggs county, on Wed. the 25th ult. at 1 o'clock P.M.,
JANETT GERTRUDE, aged 3 years 11 months 23 days. Also on Friday the
27th ult. at 7 o'clock A.M., ROBERT FREEMAN, aged 6 years 5 months
28 days, the daughter and son of Mr. Peyton and Mrs. Ruth REYNOLDS
of the above place. Were victims of Scarlet Fever.

21 Apr 1846
Died of consumption on the 6th of March last in Lee county,
MRS. HANNAH G. BUTLER, consort of Mr. Thomas Butler, of Scottsboro,
Georgia; member of the Presbyterian Church.

28 Apr 1846
Died in Monticello, Jasper county, on Thursday morning the 9th inst.,
CHARLES CARGILE, Esq., aged 82 years. Towards the close of the Rev. War,
Mr. Cargile, although a youth, took sides with the friends of
Independence and participated with them in their struggles against the
oppressions of the mother country. The war being over, he removed from
North Carolina to Wilkes county, Georgia, then on the frontiers of the
State, and was soon engaged with the other pioneers of the country in
a fierce and bloody war against the Creek Indians. He settled in Jasper
in 1807, where he lived until the time of his death; was a member of the
Legislature.

19 May 1846
Died at his residence in Russell county, Ala. on the 9th inst., of a
disease of the heart, MR. WM. GUSTAVUS CROWDER, son of the late Thos.
Crowder, of Milledgeville, Ga., in the 32d year of his age; member of
the Methodist Episcopal Church for nine years; leaves a widow, three
children and four sisters.

26 May 1846
Died in Hillsboro on the evening of the 14th inst., MRS. LUCINDA B. MORRIS,
wife of John G. Morris, and only daughter of Col. B. Bell - in the
35th year of her age.

From the Sandersville Telescope and dated Monday, May 4, 1846. A Tribute
of Respect by members of the Sandersville Bar to the memory of RUSSELL
MILLER, Esq., who departed this life on the 30th of April last.

2 June 1846
Died on the 30th ult. of Pulmonary disease at her residence in Talbot
county near Prattsburg, MRS. PRISCILLA ROUSSEAU, aged 45 years 15 days.
Mrs. Russeau was the daughter of William and Sibby Mathews and the wife
of George Rousseau (eulogy)

Died at her residence in Jasper county on the 14th ult., MRS. MARY HARRIS,
in the 66th year of her age. She lived an exemplary life in the Baptist
Church 34 years. Has left a number of children.

9 June 1846
Died at his residence in Stewart county, Geo. of Consumption on
May 26th, 1846, TOMLINSON FORT, Jr., in the 36th year of his age. He
left a wife and seven children. (eulogy)

Died in Washington county on the 2d inst. at one o'clock P.M.,
AUGUSTUS ADOLPHUS, infant son of Dr. Augustus A. and Harriet B. CULLENS,
aged 10 months 16 days.

Proclamation by Tennessee Governor Aaron V. Brown offering $500 reward
for the apprehension of James Dinning for murder committed upon the
body of WILLIAM B. NORMAN in Sumner county on the 10th day of Nov. 1845...

23 June 1846
Died in the city of Macon on the 18th inst., CLEMENTIUS DAVIS, infant
son of Col. H.G. & Mrs. M.A. LAMAR, age 3 months 18 days.

Geo. Nutter charged with the murder of JOHN A. GLOVER, a student at
Charlottesville University, has been tried and acquitted.

DR. GEORGE W. SPAULDING of Richmond, Va. committed suicide by taking
Prussic Acid on Saturday last. He is supposed to have been under the
influence of temporary mental derangement.

30 June 1846
Died at his residence in Macon on Thursdy last, DR. WILLIAM GREEN,
aged 84 years; native of Ireland; for several years filled a professor's
chair in the University of Georgia (long eulogy)

Died in Lumpkin, Ga. on the 14th instant, WILLIAM, the only son of
William A. and Eudocia FORT, aged 13 months 24 days.

14 Jul 1846
Died in this county on the 8th ult., ANN S., only child of Maj. L.S.
and Mrs. G.H. BROOKING, aged 1 year 4 months 23 days.

4 Aug 1846
Died at his uncle's residence in Irwin county, JAMES, only son of
Smith TURNER, a promising youth of 16 years 8 months 21 days.

18 Aug 1846
Died on Monday the 3d inst. at the house of Mr. and Mrs. H.P. Humphrey,
their grandchild HARRIET MARIA, aged 3 years 4 months, daughter of Hiram
and Catharine J. TYSON, formerly of this county. (short eulogy)

Died in this city on the 10th inst., GEORGE, son of Alfred M. and
Rebecca HORTON, aged 7 months 13 days.

COL. RANDOLPH PEYTON of Sumner county, Tenn., recently committed suicide
by shooting himself through the head, when in a state of temporary
alienation of mind.

25 Aug 1846
Died with congestive fever on the 11th instant in Putnam county, at
his place of residence, MR. HUGH JOHNSTON, in the 27th year of his age,
leaving a wife and two small children; member of the Baptist Church.
(eulogy)

Died at the residence of Col. Fleming Jordan near Monticello, Jasper county, Geo. on Sunday the 16th instant, MISS ELIZABETH M. CREWS, after an illness of 29 days. (Papers in Columbus and Montgomery, Ala. are requested to copy)

Died on Thursday the 7th inst. at 2 o'clock P.M. at the house of Lee Reaves, Esq., near Long's bridge in Hancock county, MRS. DEBORAH, consort of John TAYLOR, and eldest daughter of Green Anderson, Esq., of Washington county, in the 19th year of her age.

1 Sep 1846

Died on Saturday the 22d ult., DR. JOHN T. BARTOW, of Savannah, Assistant Surgeon in the Navy of the United States, in the 28th year of his age.

Died at Victoria, Texas Aug 2, in the 30th year of her age, MRS. JULIA ANN, wife of Col. Wilkins HUNT, formerly of this place, and daughter of the late George Root, formerly of Farmington, Conn.

Died on Sat. 29th August in Washington county, FREDRICK CULLENS, in his 81st year.

8 Sep 1846

Died in Irwin county on the 18th of August in the 40th year of her age, MRS. SARAH WILLCOX, wife of Capt. George Willcox of that county. She left surviving her a devoted husband and seven children to mourn.

15 Sep 1846

On Wed. night the Hon. JOHN KENNEDY, one of the Associate Justices of the Supreme court of Pennsylvania, died at his residence in Philadelphia, after a long and severe illness, in the 72d year of his age.

29 Sep 1846

Died at his residence in Sparta on Sat. morning the 16th inst., GEORGE BELL, Esq. - after a short illness.

Died in this city on Tuesday night last, FRANCES VIRGINIA, daughter of James & Frances HERTY, aged 5 weeks 2 days.

Died in Jefferson county on the morning of the 13th inst., of congestive fever, ABNER H. WRIGHT, second son of Col. Ambrose Wright, in the 19th year of his age.

Died in Macon on the 24th, Gen. W.G. SMITH, P.M. at that place.

Died at Montgomery, near Savannah, on the 9th inst., MRS. MARIA MONTGOMERY, formerly of N. York.

Melancholy suicide. The Hon. FELIX FRUNDY McCONNELL, a Representative in Congress from the State of Alabama, terminated his existence at the St. Charles Hotel, in Washington City, on the 10th instant, by literally cutting his throat from ear to ear...

6 Oct 1846

Died in Matamoras, Mexico on the 11th ult., THOS. McCRARY, a Volunteer of the Macon Guards, Georgia Regiment, formerly of this county.

Murder at Richmond. Details of the detah by shooting of D. MARVIN HOYT.
(Correspondence of the Baltimore Sun and headed Washington,
Sept. 28, 6 PM)

13 Oct 1846
Died in Putnam county on the 2nd inst., MR. CHARLES S. HURT, in the
72d year of his age.

27 Oct 1846
At the late session of the Superior Court of Green county, Warren J. Boon
and his brother Kinchen, were found guilty of the murder of JAMES H. ASLOP...
sentenced to be hung on Friday the 27th of November next.

Departed this life at his residence in Monroe county, Georgia on Friday the
2d Oct 1846, in the 88th year of his age, ROGER BERNARD MACARTHY, Esq.
He was a younger son of Charles Macarthy, Esq., Attorney at Law, and
Catharine Bernard, daughter of the Rev. F. Bernard, of Palace Ann, in the
county of Cork, Ireland. He was educated for the Bar, but having become
involved in some measure in the affair of '98, he emigrated from Ireland
in June of that year, bringing with him his first wife, the mother of the
present Charles Bernard Macarthy, Esq., of Clinton, Jones county. He landed
in New York, but soon emigrated to Savannah, where he entered into
mercantile life as a clerk with the house of Smith. His first wife seems
to have died early, and he intermarried a second time with Miss A.T. Pugh,
of the city of Savannah, by whom he left a large family, residing
principally in Bibb and Monroe counties, Georgia. After remaining in
Savannah a few years, Mr. Macarthy removed first to Sandersville, where he
became a merchant upon his own account, and afterwards to Clinton, Jones
county, where he spent the larger part of his manhood and accumulated, as
a merchant, a very handsome estate. He retired from business about 17 years
ago, and removed to the farm in Monroe county, where he died, and upon
which repose his own remains and those of his beloved wife...was educated
in the Episcopal Church at Montpelier Springs, Mr. Macarthy received
confirmation at the hands of the Bishop of the Diocese, and with his family
connected himself with St. Luke's Church.

Died recently at Mount Meigs, Ala., DR. SIMEON FULLER, formerly of
Eatonton, Geo.

Died at Macon on Sunday last, COL. ABRAHAM P. PATRICK. Col. P. was a
native of Rockingham Co., North Carolina, and was for a short time a
student of the University of that State. He had been in very delicate health
for more than a year.

Died on the 25th ult., COL. THOS. WRIGHT, at his residence in
Newton county.

10 Nov 1846
Died at his residence in Bibb county on the 27th October, TIMOTHY
MATTHEWS, Esq., in the 79th year of his age. He was a native of Halifax
county, North Carolina, but for the last fifty years a resident of this
state (eulogy)

1 Dec 1846

Died on the 18th of November at her residence four miles north of Milledgeville, MRS. CATHARINE McGEHEE, in the 75th year of her age.

Died in Twiggs Co. on the 20th Oct. last of fever complicated with pneumonia, in the 30th year of her age, MRS. ELIZABETH MARY LAND, wife of Mr. Henry Land.

8 Dec 1846

Died in Milledgeville on Sunday morning the 29th November, Major WM. F. SCOTT, aged 58 years. He was for the last 26 years a citizen of this county.

Died near Clarkesville on the 27th ult., Major JACOB WOOD, in the 78th year of his age. Was for many years President of the State Senate.

We learn from the Galveston (Texas) News of the 23d ultimo that MISS PINCKNEY FANNIN, daughter of Col. Fannin who perished in the massacre of Goliad, died in that city on the 14th.

22 Dec 1846

Died on Sat. 25th Sep last of congestive fever, COL. THOS. WRIGHT, at his residence in Newton county, aged 55 years; leaves a wife and seven children; Masonic ceremonies at funeral.

Departed this life on Monday evening 7th instant, SARAH A.P. BONNER, consort of Oliver P. Bonner, in the 26th year of her age; has left six infant children (eulogy)

Died at Savannah on the 4th inst., JOSEPH CUMMING, Esq., one of the oldest and most respected merchants of that city.

Died at his residence in Fayette county on the 3d inst., JAMES WALDRUP, in the 104th year of his age.

Died at his residence in Lowndes county (Ga.) on Monday night the 23d ult., GRIFFIN MIZEL, in the 79th year of his age.

5 Jan 1847

CAPT. HOLMES, of the Macon Volunteers. A letter from Monterey, published in the N.O. Delta, announces the decease at that place of this gallant and accomplished officer...He fell by disease, not by the hand of the enemy.

Brig. Gen. HAMER, formerly a member of Congress from Ohio, but lately in command of a Brigade of Volunteers in Mexico, has recently died at Monterey.

We regret to learn of the death of J.S DISMUKES, 2d Lieutenant of the Crawford Guards. (Columbus Times)

Hon. ALEXANDER BARROW, US Senator from Louisiana, died at Baltimore on the 29th ult. His remains were conveyed to Washington and the funeral obsequies took place on Thursday last, under direction of the Senate.

12 Jan 1847

Extraordinary trial for murder. In the Superior Court of Tennessee, last week a murder case was brought up, which is amongst the most extraordinary on record. The accused, Mrs. Mary Copeland, was convicted in the Overton Circuit Court, of the murder of RUTH DOUGHERTY...

Died in this city on the 5th inst. after a few hours illness, FANNY MARION, youngest daughter of Fred H. and Evelina R. SANFORD.

Died at Monterey (Mexico) on the 13th ult., FLEMING DAVIS, formerly of this City. He was attached to the Georgia Regiment.

Died at his residence in Jones county on the 18th of November last, MR. THOMAS W. STEWART, a native of Mecklenburg county, NC, but for the last forty years a resident of this State.

19 Jan 1847

Died in Jefferson county on the 20th ult., HON. SAMUEL B. TARVER, aged 66 years.

The Savannah Georgian of the 13th inst. says - We have this morning to announce the death of COL. EVERARD HAMILTON, one of our most respected Merchants. Col. Hamilton once filled the honorable office of Secretary of State, to which he was elected by the Legislature.

Departed this life on the 5th inst. at his residence in Elk Ridge, Anne Arundel county, Md., GENERAL CHARLES STERETT RIDGELY, in the 65th year of his age. He was the father of Captain Randolph Ridgely, who so highly distinguished himself in Mexico, and who recently died at Monterey in consequence of a fall from his horse.

Another Revolutionary soldier gone. Died on the 1st inst. at the residence of his son James M. Cason in Hancock county, Geo., MR. WILLIAM CASON, of Warren, in the 98th year of his age. Mr. C. served seven campaigns during the Rev. War - an acceptable member of the Baptist Church more than 70 years.

Death has once again visited the Senate of the United States. Judge PENNYBACKER, of Virginia, departed this life on the morning of the 12th inst....

26 Jan 1847

Funeral of CAPT. HOLMES.

Died on the 8th inst. in Russel county, Ala., MRS. MARY ANNE HARRIS, wife of Wiley J. Harris, and daughter of Randolph Mitchell, in the 22d year of her age (eulogy).

Died on the 16th inst. at his residence in Twiggs county, MR. HENRY SOLOMON, in the 54th year of his age.

Died on the 15th inst. in Eatonton, CAPT. JOHN C. MASON, in the 71st year of his age. Capt. M. was one of the first settlers of that place, a man of the strictest integrity.

2 Feb 1847

Died in Vineville on the 22d inst., MRS. MARTHA W. BAILEY, wife of
Col. Samuel T. Bailey, and eldest daughter of the Hon. Christopher B. Strong.

Twiggs Inferior Court. January Term 1847. Tribute of Respect on the death
of COL. HENRY SOLOMON who died on the 16th inst.

9 Feb 1847

Died in New Orleans on Tuesday evening 21st ult., MR. JOSEPH S. DEARING,
aged about 20 years - son of Wm. S. Dearing, Esq., of Charleston (SC). The
deceased was a volunteer in the 2d regiment of the Mississippi volunteers.

The remains of Lieutenant INGE passed through New Orleans for Mobile on the
26th ult. and were subsequently lost by the explosion of the Steam-boat that
had taken them on board.

16 Feb 1847

Died at the residence of his brother near Mt. Zion in Hancock county,
MR. MOSES WILEY, in the 74th year of his age. Was born in Mecklenburg county, NC
and came to this State with his father in 1787, a youth about 14 years of
age; from that time till his death he was a citizen of Hancock; in 1813 he
served a tour in the army under Gen. Floyd; member of Presbyterian Church.
(eulogy)

23 Feb 1847

Died in this city on Tuesday 9th inst., MRS. EMILY O. HINES, wife of
Richard K. Hines, Esq., and daughter of the late Dr. James Nisbet, in the
41st year of her age. (long eulogy) (Macon Telegraph)

Died at his residence in Jasper county on the 29th Jan. of pulmonary
consumption, MR. WM. A. REID, near the close of his fortieth year. (long eulogy)

Died at his residence in Columbia county on the 6th of February, CAPT. WILLIAM
DRANE. He was born 14 July 1765 in Prince George County, Maryland, and
emigrated to Georgia in 1786, and settled in that part of Richmond, now
Columbia County, where he resided until his death.

9 Mar 1847

Died at Macon on the 21st ult., MRS. MARY ADELINE, wife of Samuel R. BLAKE, Esq.,
in the 23d year of her age. (long eulogy)

Died at his residence in Jasper County, near Monticello, on the 14th ult.,
MERIDITH ADAMS, in the 64th year of his age; member of the Baptist Church.

16 Mar 1847

Atrocious act. On the night of the late fire, after it was nearly subdued, a
young girl by the name of COSEY, returning home with several other females,
was overtaken by a man who accosted her and, after some words, drew a pistol
and shot her in the head...the poor girl died yesterday... (Col. Times)

23 Mar 1847
>   Found dead. The Macon Messenger of the 18th inst. says - On the morning
>   of the 11th inst., a man was found dead in a small branch near the river,
>   a short distance above East Macon. His name is said to be ARCHIBALD BARLOW,
>   and that he has a family of children in or near Columbus - his age from
>   32 to 40 years. He left the house where he was staying the night previous,
>   apparently in a state of partial derangement, which was probable the cause
>   that led to his death.

6 Apr 1847
>   MRS. SARAH FRANCES LEMON departed this life at the residence of her husband
>   Alexander Lemon in McDonough, Henry County, Georgia on Saturday the 13th day
>   of March 1847. Mrs. Lemon was the youngest child of the late Joseph and
>   Rosena Denning, and was at the time of her death aged 36 years 7 days; member
>   of the Methodist Episcopal Church (long eulogy) (The Southern Christian
>   Advocate will please copy)

13 Apr 1847
>   Died at the residence of his brother-in-law James Land, Esq., in Twiggs
>   county, on the night of the 30th ult. of inflammation of the lungs after an
>   illness of six days, JAMES G. FAULK, Esq., aged 33 years 8 days. (eulogy)

20 Apr 1847
>   Died at her residence in this city at 8 o'clock A.M. on the 13th inst., after
>   a short illness, MRS. JANE MITCHELL, in the 78th year of her age, relict of
>   the late Gen. D.B. Mitchell.

>   Died on Saturday last, also in this city, MRS. PAYNE, wife of Dr. Charles J. Payne.

4 May 1847
>   Charleston Mercury relates death of HON. GEORGE C. DROMGOOLE, who expired at
>   his residence in Brunswick county, Va. on Wed. evening last, after an illness
>   of about ten days of billious fever...

>   Died at Taos, New Mexico February 7, 1847, CAPT. JOHN H.K. BURGWIN, 1st US
>   Dragoons. Capt. B. was shot in the breast with a rifle ball on the 5th of Feb.
>   in an action with the Pueblo Indians, near the town of Taos, after having
>   charged and driven them to their houses. He was a native of New Hanover county,
>   North Carolina and was educated at West Point.

>   Died on the 15th ult. at his residence in Florida, PRINCE CHARLES LOUIS
>   NAPOLEON ACHILLE MURAT, son of Joachim and Caroline Bonaparte Murat, King and
>   Queen of Naples, aged 46 years 2 months 25 days.

>   Died in New Orleans on the 24th April at half past 11 o'clock P.M., CAPT.
>   ALEXANDER J. SWIFT, of the U.S. Corps of Engineers.

11 May 1847
>   JOSIAH HUDGINS was executed in Forsyth, Monroe county, on Friday 30th ult.
>   for the murder of his overseer, John Anderson, in 1845.

18 May 1847

HON. JESSE SPEIGHT, U.S. Senator from Mississippi, recently died at his residence near Columbus. He was a native of North Carolina, and removed to Mississippi in 1837.

Died at Forsyth, Monroe county, on Sunday evening the 9th inst., MRS. MARY E. TUCKER, consort of H.H. Tucker, Esq., and daughter of Dr. Charles West, of Houston county, aged about 24 years.

Died in Hancock county on the 27th ult., MRS. ELIZA, wife of Presley HARPER, Esq., and daughter of Lott Harton, Esq., aged 34 years.

25 May 1847

Died at her residence in Houston county on the 11th instant, MRS. GATSEY ANN PRINGLE, wife of James Adger Pringle, and youngest child of Joel and Nancy Loftin, in the 23d year of her age. She has left behind her one child too young to know its loss... (short eulogy)

1 June 1847

Died at Augusta, Benton county, Florida, on the 13th April of dropsy, CO. JOSIAH S. PATTERSON; for some years a prominent member of the Georgia bar; ...laboring under the impression that his disease was consumption, he removed to Southern Florida with the hope of restoration. (Eufaula Democrat)

Died in this city of Typhus Fever on Friday the 28th ult., MR. WILLIAM P. BROOKS, of the county of Twiggs, Georgia, in the 66th year of his age; an acceptable member of the Baptist Church.

Died in Macon on the 19th ult., JONATHAN HUGHES, infant son of Wm. B. and C.A. HARRISON, aged 2 months 14 days.

Died at the residence of his nephew's Henry E. Everitte in Twiggs county, on the 8th of May, JORDAN W. LEE, aged 45 years. Has left behind six orphans...

Convicted. Jones Butler was found guilty last week in Muscogee county of the murder of MARY ANN COURSIE and was to have been sentenced to death yesterday...

8 June 1847

Died at the residence of his father in Jasper county on Sunday night the 16th ult., LEVI C. DANIEL, oldest son of Mr. Robert H. Daniel, in the 21st year of his age.

Died at his residence in Girard, Ala., JAMES C. McGIBONEY, on Sunday morning 23d ult., in the 51st year of his age, formerly of Green county, Ga.

Sad accident. We learn that on Sat. last, Mr. White, of the firm of White & Headon of Decatur, while driving a pair of horses in a Barouche from Atlanta to Decatur, when within sight of the village the horses took fright, and being unmanageable precipitated over the dash board MISS STONE, daughter of Daniel Stone, and old and respectable citizen and the Clerk of the Superior Court of Decatur, the Barouche passing over and crushing her head most horribly, which resulted in her death immediately. (Constitutionalist, June 2d)

15 June 1847
    Death of WM. LEE, Esq. He died on Sunday the 30th ult. at the residence of
    his nephew and son-in-lae Professor Stephen Lee, near Ashville, North
    Carolina, in the 70th year of his age. Was formerly a member of the State
    Legislature from this city, and was for many years a Teller in the Bank of
    the State of South Carolina. Was a brother of the late and learned Judge
    Lee. (Charleston Courier)

22 June 1847
    Died on the 5th inst. at his residence in Putnam county, N.L. WALKER, in
    the 74th year of his age.

    Died in Putnam county on the 13th inst., MRS. MARY E. VASSER, in the
    82d year of her age.

    Died on the 4th instant in the 36th year of his age, MR. CARY SOLOMON, of
    Marion, Twiggs county.

29 June 1847
    Died at his residence in Athens, Geo. on Wed. June 16, 1847, JAMES CAMAK, Esq.,
    aged 52 years.

    Died on the 18th inst. at 2 o'clock P.M. at her father's residence at
    Etowah Works, Cass county, Georgia, MISS CAMILLA C. COOPER, daughter of
    Mark A. and Sophronia A.R. Cooper, aged 17 years.

    The Mobile Register of the 15th inst. says - The county and city are full of
    excitement on account of the tragedy in Sumter county. The only particulars
    that we deem authentic and fit for publication are that John Anthony Winston,
    late State Senator in the late Legislature and President of the State Senate,
    and a candidate for re-election in August, shot DR. S.S. PERRY, of the same
    county on the ___ inst. and wounded him mortally, so that he died within an
    hour...

6 July 1847
    Brutal murder. A villain incarnate. A daughter seduced. Her father and
    brother conwardly murdered! A most brutal murder, says our informant, of a
    father and son, was perpetrated at Pine Bluffs, Arkansas by a Doctor Emory
    upon the bodies of JAMES DeBAUN, Senior and his son JAMES DeBAUN, Junior.
    Dr. E. was the family physician of Mr. DeBaun, and in his professional
    intercourse seduced the daughter of Mr. DeBaun... (N.O. Delta)

    Fatal rail road accident. On Sat. morning last about 20 minutes before five
    o'clock, as the Passenger train on the Central Rail Road got within a fourth
    of a mile of the 117 mile post, the Engine "Oglethorpe" with tender, baggage
    and passenger cars all precipitated off the track into a cavity, caused by a
    very heavy and unprecedented rain which fell during Friday night...
    OLIVER B. DARBY, fireman, native of Washington county, was instantly killed.
    JOHN LONG, fireman, native of Ireland and resident of Savannah, was so injured
    that he survived but four hours. CHARLES T. ENGLAND, runner, formerly of
    Baltimore, Maryland, was so mangled and scalded that he survived but eight
    hours. Mr. England has left a sister in Macon, whither his remains were
    conveyed for interment. Mr. Darby has left a mother and sister. Mr. Long left
    no family. (Sav. Georgian)

20 July 1847

Death of COL. A.H. PEMBERTON, the former editor and proprietor of the South Carolinian. Mr. P. died at his residence near this place on yesterday afternoon about 4 o'clock, after a protracted illness. Mr. P. has been connected with the press, both in this State and Georgia for a number of years. (Columbia South Carolinian of Tuesday)

27 July 1847

Died on Wed. morning the 14th inst. of Billious Fever, MRS. LUCY ANN FRANCES BROWN, wife of Mr. Oscar V. Brown, and eldest daughter of Col. A.W. and Mrs. Susan R. Redding of this city, in the 18th year of her age; leaves a husband, parents, brothers and sisters; member of the Methodist Episcopal Church - joined in her 12th year. (long eulogy)

Died at Macon on Thursday last after a short illness, DR. RICHARD H. RANDOLPH, aged about 51 years; member of the Presbyterian Church. (long eulogy)

3 Aug 1847

Died of the Typhus Fever at his residence in Butts county, in the 29th year of his age, COL. ROBERT F. DOUGLASS, the last surviving son and child of the Rev. Francis Douglass; leaves his father and mother, a disconsolate widow, and three lovely children...on 18th inst. his remains were conducted to the family graveyard and interred with Masonic honors - funeral discourse by Rev. Meshack Lowry. (eulogy)

Departed this life on the 17th ult., MRS. LUCY ANN WHITFIELD, consort of Mr. Benjamin F. Whitfield, of Jasper, and eldest daughter of Alexander C. Maddox, Esq., of Putnam county, aged 17 years 7 months.

Departed this life on Wed. the 21st ult., MRS. SARAH T. HUNT, wife of Thos. Hunt, Esq., of Jones County, and daughter of the late Jesse McKinne Pope, deceased, in the 44th year of her age; leaves husband and twelve children, one of whom (an infant daughter) was only one hour and a half old.

10 Aug 1847

Died at her residence in Baldwin county on Sunday evening the 25th ult. after an illness of several months, MRS. ELIZABETH GREEN, in the 73d year of her age; member of the Methodist Episcopal Church. (eulogy)

24 Aug 1847

Departed this life at the General Hospital, New Orleans Barracks, ORRIN W., youngest son of Samuel and Mary BUFFINGTON, of Milledgeville, aged 22 years 10 months. He was admitted to the Hospital May 27, 1847 completely emaciated and prostrated from chronic diarrhea - he lingered until June 4th when he died; was a member of Company of Capt. Holmes, Georgia Regiment.

7 Sep 1847

The papers of New York announce the death of HON. SILAS WRIGHT. He died at his residence in Canton, St. Laurence county, of apoplexy on the 27th ult., aged 55 years...

109

14 Sep 1847

Departed this life at her father's residence in Hayneville, Houston county, Ga., after a protracted and painful illness, MISS SARAH EVELYN WEST, daughter of Dr. Charles and Mrs. Sarah Evelyn West, aged 17 years 8 months. Had united with the Presbyterian Church in Macon while a pupil in the Female College.

21 Sep 1847

Died on the evening of the 5th inst. at her residence in Monticello, of Puerperal fever, MRS. CAROLINE E. VARNER, wife of Samuel D. Varner, and daughter of Jeremiah and Mary Pearson, aged 18 years 6 months 19 days; leaves husband and infant daughter. (eulogy) (Constitutionalist and Macon papers will please copy)

28 Sep 1847

Died of Congestive fever on Friday the 17th inst. at the residence of her grandfather Spencer Crane, Esq., in the vicinity of Monticello, on the third day of her illness, REBECCA, daughter of William and Catharine A. MARKS, of Montgomery, Ala., aged 10 years 6 months 5 days. (eulogy) (Montgomery papers will please copy)

Died at his residence in Putnam county on the 12th inst., MR. HENRY HUNTER, in the 58th year of his age. He has left three sons an early orphanage, their mother having died two years previous.

Died at Midway on Sunday morning last, ELIZABETH DELAUNEY, daughter of Mr. and Mrs. Otis CHILDS, aged 22 months.

12 Oct 1847

Departed this life in Irwin county on the 17th ult., MISS MARTHA MOBLEY, in the 17th year of her age. (eulogy)

Died in this city on the 27th ult. of Dropsy of the chest, MRS. EMILY BECKHAM, consort of Mr. Simon Beckham, and daughter of Mr. William Brooks, late of Twiggs county, deceased, in the 21st year of her age; member of the Baptist Church. (eulogy)

Died of Typhus Fever on Friday the 24th of September at the residence of Thomas S. Chappel, in Twiggs county, MARY M. GIBSON, daughter of Samuel and Sarah L. Bragg of Wilkinson county, aged 18 years 9 months 26 days.

19 Oct 1847

Died at Richmond Bath on Monday the 11th inst., in the 62d year of his age, DR. JAMES WHITEHEAD.

The Columbia Temperance Advocate of yesterday brings us the melancholy news of the death of the HON. WILLIAM HARPER, who expired at his residence in Fairfield district, South Carolina on Sunday last. In his death the bench of South Carolina has lost her greatest jurist... (Charleston Mercury, 15th inst.)

26 Oct 1847

Departed this life on the 14th inst. of Typhus Fever, at the residence of his mother in Hancock county, MR. BURWELL NEWTON BASS, in the 27th year of his age; was born, raised and educated in the county of Hancock (eulogy)

2 Nov 1847

Died at Grand Collion at the residence of his uncle William S. Mayfield, in Terre Bonne parish, La., WILLIAM LOWNDES FREEMAN, 2d Aug 1847, 10 minutes past 5 o'clock P.M., after a severe and painful illness of three weeks of acute inflammation of the liver. William was born 25th Jan 1830 and thus was 17 years 6 months 8 days old. He left the family roof at the tender age of a little under 15 years old, under melancholy and very afflicting circumstances, though not of a dishonorable character. William was the son of Dr. Henry Freeman of Carnesville, Georgia, where his unfortunate son was born and raised; imbued with religious sentiments, on the death of his mother in the spring of 1846... (eulogy)

9 Nov 1847

Died at his residence in Stewart county, Georgia on the 6th of October, LEWIS MILLER, in the 81st year of his age. Was born in New York; his father removed when he was quite young to North Carolina and settled near Guilford, and remained there during the revolution; he being the eldest son, it devolved on him to make a support with his mother's assistance in consequence of his father' being engaged in that trying epoch for independence; he removed from there to Georgia and settled in Washington county, and lived there for more than 40 years; and ten years ago he removed to Stewart county; for more than 50 years a member of the Baptist Church and served more than 40 years as deacon; leaves widow and six children.

Departed this life at the house of Thomas Hunt, Esq. in Jones county on Sunday the 24th of October last, his eldest son WM. M. HUNT, in the 22d year of his age. (long eulogy)

12 Nov 1847 - Extra

Died in Jones county on the 28th October at 1 o'clock A.M., SAM'L. T. STEWART, infant son of T.J. & M.J. Stewart, aged 6 months 23 days.

Also, of Typhus Fever on the same day at 7 o'clock P.M., MARTHA J. STEWART, consort of Thos. J. Stewart and daughter of Benj. & Sarah Finney, aged 22 years 1 month 17 days. Mrs. Atewart has left an affectionate husband to whom she had been united only 15 months.

16 Nov 1847

Departed this life at Tampico, in Mexico, in the 25th year of his age, DR. JOSEPH EDWARD WALTHALL, son of Col. Turman Walthall of Butts county, Georgia. He was graduated at the Medical College of Georgia at Augusta in 1844, and settled at Cahawba, Ala. When the war broke out in Mexico in May 1846, he volunteered in Capt. ____ company at Cahawba...was appointed assistant Surgeon of the Port of Tampico and had just arrived and entered upon the duties of his appointment when on 18th Sept he was taken with the prevailing epidemic Yellow Fever and died on 21st following at 6 o'clock in the morning.

Died at Clinton, Anderson county, E. Tennessee, on the 14th of Oct of Billious Fever, THOMAS J. WALTHALL, brother of Dr. Walthall, in the 19th year of his age. He was a student at E. Tennessee University at Knoxville, and during Vacation, he went to Clinton, 18 miles from Knoxville, for the purpose of pursuing his studies in Mathematics at the Academy at that place. (With Tributes of Respect by Phi Delta Society and Sophomore Class of E. Tennessee University)

A young gentleman named CRAWFORD, a son of the late Hon. W. H. Crawford, of Georgia, and a member of the Jefferson Medical School of Philadelphia, came to his death a few days ago in that city from the effects of a slight puncture received in dissecting.

Died in the harness. Last evening as the REV. MR. TAPPAN, chaplain of the Alms House, was concluding his opening prayer in the chapel of the institution, during Divine Service, his voice faltered and he suddenly fell in the pulpit in an apoplectic fit... (New York Com. Adv.)

19 Nov 1847 - Extra

Died at his residence in Upson county, Ga. on the 29th of October last, in the 49th year of his age, the REV. JOHN BARKER, a devoted member of the Baptist Church for 12 or 14 years; leaves wife and children. (The Recorder and Jour. & Messenger will please copy)

Died at Mount Yonah, Ga. on the evening of the 5th inst., of Croup, EMILY TURMAN, youngest daughter of Wm. B. and Elizabeth SHELTON, aged 6 months 24 days. (The Constitutionalist will please copy)

30 Nov 1847

Death of ALLEN A. CHANDLER. Letter headed Camp near Mear, Mexico and dated August 8, 1847 and addressed to Mr. Asa Chandler of Fayette county, Ga. ...painful duty to announce to you the death of your beloved son, ALLEN A. CHANDLER. He was drowned at Reinosa, in the Rio Grande, on the 25th of July. He had gone in to bathe with the boys from Fayette, and was persuaded by them to attempt to swim the river...

21 Dec 1847

MILTON HOMER GATHRIGHT died at one o'clock P.M. on Friday last. With the first settlement of our Cherokee country - with the organization of its courts - with its education system - with almost every important improvement in its roads and bridges - the name of Gathright is connected... (Dahlonega Watchman, 16th instant)

Death of COL. ECHOLS who had long and ably served the State in her legislative counsels, and for many years had officiated as President of the Senate. Was placed by the President of the United States at the head of a regiment in the regular service, he went forth to meet his country's enemy. He died in the enemy's territory... (from Constitutionalist of 19th inst.)

28 Dec 1847

HON. ROGER L. GAMBLE died at his residence in Jefferson county on the 22d inst. of apoplexy; for many years a representative in the State Legislature, and afterwards in the Congress of the United States.

4 Jan 1848

Died on the 16th ult., HENRY GOLDEN, youngest son of John R. and Caroline R. BOSTICK, aged 14 months.

Died at Broughton Island, near Darien, very suddenly on the 23d ult., MRS. FLORIDA BRYAN, wife of Hon. Thomas M. Forman, and daughter of Hon. Geo. M. Troup.

HON. JOHN FAIRFIELD, Ex-Governor of Maine and Senator from that State, died at Washington City on the 24th ult.

11 Jan 1848

Died at the residence of Isaac Newell in this place on Sat. 8th inst., MR. JOHN M. PATTON, Secretary of the Executive Department, in the 21st year of his age.

18 Jan 1848

Died in Milledgeville on Sat. the 8th inst. of Typhoid Pneumonia, MR. JOHN M. PATTON, son of Dr. Robert H. Patton, of Cassville, and Secretary in the Executive Department of Georgia - aged 20 years 9 months 10 days. (long eulogy) (Cassville Pioneer)

25 Jan 1848

Died at Mr. Benj. Lester's in Baldwin county on the 17th inst., ELLA COLUMBIA, daughter and only child of Benj. J. and Mississippi A. LESTER, aged 11 months 18 days (short eulogy).

8 Feb 1848

Died January 30th, 1848 at his residence in Glennville, Ala., of compression of the brain from extravasated blood, CAPT. JULIUS C.B. MITCHELL, in the 53d year of his age. (long eulogy)

Died in this city on Friday the 4th inst. at half past 10 o'clock, A.M., MR. JOSEPH STOVALL, Sen., in the 61st year of his age.

HON. J.W. JONES, former speaker of the House of Representatives, died at his residence in Chesterfield, Virginia, on the 29th ult...

15 Feb 1848

Died at Chunynuggee, Ala., the residence of Dr. N.B. Powell, MRS. CARTER, the wife of James Carter, Esq., formerly of this city, and the daughter of Dr. Powell.

22 Feb 1848

Departed this life at her residence in this place on the 19th inst., MRS. VIRGINIA DUBOURG, aged 48 years; member of the Presbyterian Church. (short eulogy)

Died on Tuesday the 15th inst. at about 3 o'clock P.M. at his residence in Monroe county, Ga., MR. JOSEPH HEARD, in the 75th year of his age.

29 Feb 1848

Died of Pneumonia at the residence of her son-in-law Rev. Ferdinand Jacobs, near Milledgeville, on Monday Feb 14th, MRS. ABIGAIL O. RIPLEY, relict of the late Hon. Jas. Wheelock Ripley of Maine.

7 Mar 1848

Died at his residence in Harris County, Ga. on the 12th of Feb 1848 of Apoplexy, MR. LEWIS J. DOWDELL, in the 63d year of his age. Was a native of Virginia. While he was but a boy, his father emigrated to Kentucky - from which State in maturer life he moved to Georgia and settled in Jasper county. For several years past he has resided in Harris County. He buried his wife in Jasper in 1826, whither at his own request...his children have conveyed his remains to be deposited at the side of her grave. (eulogy)

14 Mar 1848

Died at his residence in Morgan County on the 15th of Feb. last, JOSEPH HEARD, in the 76th year of his age.

Died at Washington at 5 o'clock, of the evening of the 4th of March, HENRY JACKSON, son of the Hon. Howell COBB, of Georgia, aged 3 years 9 months 18 days.

21 Mar 1848

CHARLES SHERWOOD, Esq., U.S. Consul at Messine, Sicily, died in that city on the 2d January last. Mr. Sherwood was formerly a lawyer in New York.

Another death from chloroform. In New York on Tuesday an inquest was held on the body of PATRICK MURPHY...

Death of a member of Congress. The Savannah Republican of Tuesday says - We some time since (20th December) recorded the arrival here of the Hon. J. M. HOLLEY, M.C., from the state of N. York, on his way to Florida for his health. We regret to learn his recent death from hemorrhage of the lungs.

28 Mar 1848

Died at the plantation of Maj. Richard Rowell in Baldwin county, of Paralysis, on Sat. the 18th inst., ABNER LOCKE, in the 63d year of his age.

4 Apr 1848

The Savannah papers of Monday the 28th ult. came to us clad in mourning on account of the death of FRANCIS WINTER, Esq., one of the proprietors of the Republican. He died after a short illness at the age of 34 years.

11 Apr 1848

Died at his residence in Monroe county on the 30th of March, MR. ROBERT WHATLEY, aged 75 years...But his disease being Pneumonia complicated with Quinzy... (short eulogy) (Columbus Times, Constitutionalist, and Georgian will please copy)

The Hon. MR. BLACK, Rep. in Congress from South Carolina, died at Washington on the evening of the 3d instant.

18 Apr 1848

Melancholy accident. A truly melancholy occurrence took place on our Rail Road at an early hour yesterday morning. The engine "Buena Vista," to which was attached a train of freight cars, left Hamburg on her downward passage, but when in the vicinity of the 34 mile post, the engine exploded; and, we regret to add, that her engineer, MR. GEO. M. ARTOPE, JR., his assistant, MR. HENRY W. CAMMER, and a fireman were killed by the explosion... (Courier)

25 Apr 1848

Died at the residence of her father James McCune, Esq., in Butts county, Ga. April 7th, 1848, MRS. ADALINE M. McMICHAEL, in the 23d year of her age...but scarce one year of her married life had elapsed, ere the ruthless messenger death marker her for his victim...member of the Methodist Church. (eulogy)

2 May 1848

Departed this life on the 27th ult. at her father's in Baldwin county, MISS LOUIZA J., aged 14 years 11 days, daughter of the Rev. Michael LEONARD.

9 May 1848

Died near Jackson in Butts county, Ga. April 20 after a short but severe illness, MRS. MARTHA HARKNESS, wife of James W. Harkness and daughter of Richard and Lucy Boyd, aged 27 years; member of the Baptist Church. (eulogy)

Died of pneumonia in Twiggs county Feb. 6, 1848, MRS. LUCRETIA LAND, in the 31st year of her age; member of the Methodist Church; commended her three little children to the care of her step-mother; her husband preceded her in death only a few weeks. (eulogy)

Sen. ASHLEY, of Arkansas, died at Washington city on the 30th ult. He was Chairman of the Judiciary Committee.

Proclamation by Gov. George W. Towns offering reward of $100 each for the apprehension of William B. Hendrix and William B. Nations for the murder committed upon the body of WILLIAM P. GOODWIN in Lumpkin county on the 5th day of February last...

16 May 1848

Died on the 10th inst. at home three miles from this city, in the 28th year of her age, MRS. ELIZA A., wife of Col. Samuel BUFFINGTON, JR., and daughter of Col. John Bozeman, formerly of this place; leaves husband and four small children; member of M.E. Church (long eulogy)

23 May 1848

Died at his residence in Stewart county, Ga. on the morning of the 6th inst., MR. WILLIAM B. CABANISS, in the 26th year of his age.

Died at his residence in Baldwin county on the 30th of April, MR. BENJAMIN L. LESTER. He has left a widow and three small children to mourn his loss.

Died at his residence in Butts county on the 14th inst., ROBERT GRIER, aged about 63 years. The deceased has been known to the people of Georgia and South Carolina as the author of Astronomical calculations for the meridians of these states.

Died at Decatur on the 19th inst. at 4 o'clock P.M., VIRGIL WORD MURPHY, only son of C. & Catherine Murphy, aged 5 weeks 2 days.

Died suddenly at Sandy Ridge in Lowndes county on the 19th inst., COL. ANDREW J. LAMAR, formerly of Georgia. (Montgomery, Ala. Journal)

RICHARD H. TOLER, Esq., the able and accomplished editor of the Richmond (Va) Whig, died on the 15th inst., aged 49 years.

Another tragedy. On Friday last a fatal rencountre took place at Starkville, Lee county, between Dr. E.V. Monroe and JAS. A. MACON, which resulted in the immediate death of the latter... (Albany Courier, 19th inst.)

30 May 1848

Details of the death of ALFRED ANDERSON PARK, familiarly called by his friends "Chilly Park" from his strong resemblance to the Indian Chief, Chilly McIntosh...served in war with Mexico; died on Friday the 26th day of May at the Indian Springs in Butts county, aged nearly 25 years. (Savannah, Macon, Augusta, Columbia and Madison papers, please copy)

Died in this city in the evening of the 19th inst., MR. JOHN UNDERWOOD, in the 26th year of his age. Was a native of Milledgeville, Ga. but a resident of this city since 1845. The cause of his melancholy death was a fracture of the head, which he received by being thrown from a vehicle in which he was riding. (eulogy) (Montgomery Journal)

Notice of the death of Rev. ASHBEL GREEN, of Philadelphia, the oldest Presbyterian minister in the United States...

13 June 1848

Died at Midway near this city on Thursday morning last, aged about 56 years, THOMAS H. HALL, Esq., late Cashier of the Bank of Milledgeville. Was a native of Pennsylvania but for the last 28 years a citizen of Georgia; a member of the Presbyterian Church (eulogy).

Died on Thursday last at the Indian Spring, COL. HENRY F. YOUNG, of this city, aged 48 years. Was born in North Carolina and reared in Tennessee. At the age of 18, he entered the service of his country, under Gen. Jackson in the Seminole campaign of 1818...has resided at Greensboro, Augusta and Madison, but for the last 15 or 20 years this city has been his permanent abode. Was interred by the Masonic Lodge of Butts county. (Georgia and Tennessee papers please copy)

20 June 1848

Departed this life on Monday the 29th of May, a few minutes after 10 o'clock P.M. at the residence of her husband, one mile from Lafayette, Walker Co., Ga., in the 49th year of her age, of complicated disease, MRS. REBECCA FARIS, consort of Col. Samuel Faris; member of the Methodist Church (eulogy).

27 June 1848

A great and good man has fallen. Announcement of the sudden death of Rev. THOMAS GOULDING, D.D., the venerable Pastor of the Presbyterian Church of this city...was 62 years of age on the 14th of last March, nearly two-thirds of his life having been passed in the work of the Ministry; leaves an aged wife and eight children. (Muscogee Democrat, 22d inst.)

4 July 1848

Died at the residence of his father in Stewart county on the 10th ult., in the 19th year of his age, JAS. L. HOUSE; for the last four years an exemplary member of the Methodist Episcopal Church.

11 July 1848

Died in this county of Measles on Tuesday the 9th of May 1848, JAMES MONTGOMERY, in the 85th year of his age. He was born and raised in Orange county, North Carolina, and emograted to Georgia in the 28th year of his age...was raised an Episcopalian but never experienced true religion until about the fortieth year of his age...lived a faithful and consistent member of the Methodist Episcopal Church near twenty years (eulogy)

18 July 1848

Died at Hillsboro, Ga. on Sunday evening the 18th day of June 1848,
JOHN G. MORRIS, in the 35th year of his age; has left three orphan
children.

Died in Meriwether county of Typhoid Fever on the evening of the third
instant, ANDREW JACKSON, in the 19th year of his age, eldest son of
Hinson N. and Olive Jackson. (eulogy)

Died in Crawford county on the 2d inst., MARY, infant and only daughter
of Capt. John W. and Mrs. Elizabeth DENT, in the 5th year of her age.
(Columbus Enquirer and West Tennessee Whig will please copy)

Proclamation by Gov. George W. Towns offering $150 reward for the
apprehension of Henry Tuggle for the murder of his wife MARY ANN TUGGLE
in Forsyth county on the 10th day of April last...also charged with having
made attempt to rape Eliza Tuggle...

25 July 1848

Died on the 20th inst. at the residence of Walter H. Mitchell of this place,
in the 77th year of her age, MRS. MARGARET ALEXANDER, relict of Abden
Alexander, formerly of Jasper county. (eulogy)

Died in Louisiana on the 19th of June last, MRS. MARY JAMES RANDLE, consort
of E.W. Randle, and eldest daughter of the late Joseph Stovall of this
city. (eulogy)

1 Aug 1848

GOV. SHUNK, who a few weeks since resigned the Executive Chair of
Pennsylvania on account of his health, died at Harrisburg on the 22d ult.

Proclamation by Gov. George W. Towns offering $100 reward for the apprehension
of William H. Sterling for murder committed upon the body of JONATHAN GLANTON
in Upson County on the 26th day of July last...

5 Sep 1848

SARAH W. FANNIN, of the city of Savannah, departed this life after a
protracted illness on the 28th July last at North Hampton, Mass., in the
25th year of her age. Was the eldest daughter of Col. A.B. Fannin.

12 Sep 1848

We are pained to announce the death of Judge HENRY ST. GEORGE TUCKER at
his residence in Winchester on Monday morning, August 28... (Richmond Enquirer)

26 Sep 1848

Died on the 19th inst. at the residence of Col. D.C. Campbell, at Midway
near this city, in the 72d year of her age, MRS. ANN E. GEDDES, relict of
the late Robert Geddes, Esq., of Charleston. She was a native of South
Carolina, and for the greater part of her life a resident of Charleston;
for nearly thirty years a member of the Presbyterian Church.

The Baltimore Sun announces the death of Commodore ALEXANDER SLIDELL
McKENZIE, U.S.N.

3 Oct 1848

Died on the 19th ult. in Wilbraham, Mass., MARY LOWRIE, eldest daughter of Mr. & Mrs. Otis CHILDS of this place, aged 6 years 11 months (eulogy).

Died in Pulaski county September 21st of congestive remittent fever, JULIUS TENNILLE JORDAN, son of Burwell and Lavinia W. Jordan, aged 3 years 8 months 9 days.

Proclamation by Gov. George W. Towns offering $150 reward for the apprehension of William Terrell for murder committed upon the body of JAMES McWILLIAMS in DeKalb County on the 14th September instant...

17 Oct 1848

Died at Rotherwood, Carroll county, Ga. on the 12th Sept., MRS. ELIZA B. NAPIER, wife of Thomas T. Napier, Esq., within a few days of the 39th year of her age (long eulogy - mentions the loss of her only and beloved daughter)

24 Oct 1848

Died at his residence in Cass county on the 30th ult., GEN. CHARLES H. NELSON, in the 53d year of his age...his constitution having suffered from six campaigns in Florida...in Mexican War as head of a company in the late Battalion of Mounted Volunteers from Georgia.

31 Oct 1848

The Charleston papers of Friday last announce the decease of Hon. DIXON H. LEWIS, distinguished Senator from Alabama. He died at N. York on the day preceding.

7 Nov 1848

Died in this city on Sunday evening 8 o'clock 5th inst., MRS. EMILY M. WILLIAMSON, consort of Maj. Wm. T. Williamson, aged 34 years 5 months; for the last eight years of her life she was a devoted member of the Presbyterian Church.

Departed this life on the 23d inst. at the residence of A.P. Peacock in this county, after twenty three days confinement from a wound received by falling from a horse, JOHN PEACOCK, senr., aged 82 years 8 months 12 days. Was a native of North Carolina but for the last forty years a citizen of Washington county.

Long eulogy on the death of HON. DIXON H. LEWIS.

The corpse of Ex-Governor McNUTT, of Mississippi, says the Memphis Enquirer of the 24th, arrived in this city last night, we presume on its passage to his residence at Jackson, Miss. We are informed that he died on Sunday night at Cockrum's Cross Roads, after a short sickness of an inflammatory character...

21 Nov 1848

Died suddenly at the residence of Capt. Francis Ross on the evening of the 10th inst., COL. JOHN BOZEMAN, in the 56th year of his age; member of M.E. Church; leaves a deeply afflicted wife who is far from her native Green Mountain home. (eulogy) (Editors in Geo., Fla., and Miss. will please copy)

Man burnt to death. On Thursday evening last a most melancholy accident occurred near Kennett Square, Chester county, Pa. An old gentleman named JAMES HOLLAND, between 70 and 80 years of age, during the absence of his family, as he was in the habit of doing, had entered his barn, as is supposed with a light, for the purpose of procuring feed for his hogs; and by some means unknown, the hay or straw caught fire from the candle, and in a few minutes the building was in a blaze. The barn together with about one hundred bushels of grain, was totally destroyed, and sad to relate the old gentleman was consumed in the same.

Proclamation by Gov. George W. Towns offering $150 reward for the apprehension of George Bassett for murder committed upon the body of ISAAC SEWELL in Bibb County on the evening of the 11th instant...

Proclamation by Gov. George W. Towns offering $100 reward for the apprehension of Jackson Sawyers for murder committed upon the body of WILLIAM R. LESTER in Stewart County on the 7th instant...

19 Dec 1848
Proclamation by Gov. George W. Towns offering $150 reward for the apprehension of Robert Flewellen for murder committed upon the body of URIAH T. LOCKETT in Monroe County on the 28th day of September last...

9 Jan 1849
Died in this city on Monday evening January 1st, MRS. SARAH ANN, consort of Mr. Wm. BARNES, in the 37th year of her age. Was a native of Boston, Massachusetts.

16 Jan 1849
Died very suddenly on the 9th instant at Fortville, MRS. MARY GOODWIN, consort of Col. Thomas MOUGHON and eldest daughter of the late Capt. Sanford, in the 59th year of her age. (short eulogy)

Died at his residence in Washington county on the 6th inst. of a painful and lingering disease, NATHANIEL G. PACE, in the 70th year of his age. (eulogy) (Columbus Enquirer and Eufaula papers will please copy)

A telegraphic despatch from the West was received at Washington yesterday, announcing the death of HON. A.H. SEVIER, late Minister to Mexico, and for many years Representative and Senator from the State of Arkansas. (Charleston Mercury, 10th inst)

Hon. JAMES DELLET, late a Representative to Congress, from Alabama, died at Claiborne, Dec. 21st. He was a native of South Carolina.

23 Jan 1849
Died at his residence in Perry, Houston county, on Wed. last, JAMES M. KELLY, Esq., in the 52nd year of his age; for several years he represented with ability the county of Houston in the Senate and House of Rep. and upon the organization of the Supreme Court, he received the appointment of Reporter of its decisions. That office he held at the time of his death; mentions the three volumes of "Kelly's Reports."

Died of violent congestion of the Lungs, near Monticello in Jasper county, on the 3d ult., MRS. MARY WILLIAMS McMICHAEL, consort of Capt. Shadrach McMichael, in the 63d year of her age; for more than forty years a consistent member of the Baptist Church. (short eulogy)

Died on Monday afternoon the 1st inst. at her son's residence in Baldwin county, of paralysis, MRS. SUSANNAH GUERINEAU, formerly of Savannah, but for the last nine years a resident of the above county.

Died in Baldwin county on the 15th inst., JAMES B. FRANKLIN, the only son of Mr. James and Petience PULLY, aged 3 years 6 months 15 days.

30 Jan 1849

Died in Houston County on the 20th inst., SARAH JANE, daughter of John S. and Sarah TAYLOR, in the 10th year of her age.

6 Feb 1849

Died in Crawford county on the 2d inst., ISAAC DENNIS, SR., in the 66th year of his age. (short eulogy)

Murder of the O'NEAL family in Overton County...Patsy A. Troxdale, Nicholas Stevens, and Wm. E. Upton were indicted and convicted in Overton county for the murder of the O'Neal family, consisting of the father and mother and five children, embracing the whole family except Patsy A. Troxdale, who was a daughter of old O'Neal... (Nashville Union)

20 Feb 1849

CAPT. AUGUSTUS L. SHEPPARD, of the 8th Infantry, U.S. Army, died suddenly on the 22d ult. at Jefferson Barracks.

27 Feb 1849

CAPT. SAMUEL TRASK, a soldier of the revolution, aged 99 years 9 months, died at Roxbury, Mass. on Wed. of last week.

The Macon Journal and Messenger of the 21st inst. says - We regret to announce the death of HON. E.D. TRACY, which took place at his residence in this city yesterday morning. Judge Tracy was a native of Connecticut but had resided in this city for nearly a quarter of a century.

6 Mar 1849

Died very suddenly on Wed. the 28th inst., LAURA BEECHER, eldest daughter of Dr. Geo. D. CASE of this city, aged 5 years 5 months.

20 Mar 1849

Died in Scottsboro, Ga. on the 13th inst. after a sickness of nine days from Pneumonia, WM. M. PRESCOTT, JR., son of Wm. M. Prescitt, Esq., of Washington, Louisiana. Was a member of the Junior Class of Oglethorpe University, and 17 years of age. (long eulogy)

27 Mar 1849

MRS. SUSAN C. WHITAKER, wife of Samuel C. Whitaker and youngest daughter of Mr. Geo. and Mrs. Mary Murph, died in Scottsborough of Typhoid pneumonia on Sat. morning the 23d inst., aged 26 years 1 day. She joined the Methodist E. Church in Milledgeville in 1839; leaves an aged father and mother and three little children. (eulogy)

3 Apr 1849

Died in this city on the 19th of March of Whooping-cough, MISS MARY WINEFRIED, eldest daughter of Mr. Nathan and Mrs. M.P. HAWKINS, aged 10 years 14 days.

HON. BENJAMIN A. BIDLACK, United States Charge d'Affairs near the Government of New Granada, died at Bogota on the 6th January last.

10 Apr 1849

From the Journal & Messenger. Melancholy intelligence. We have been favoured with the perusal of a letter post-marked at Cotile, Louisiana, and dated on the 9th of February, which gives the most melancholy, heart rending intelligence, in regard to a company of emigrants from Monroe County, Ga. The party, consisting of 34 whites and 43 negroes, left Monroe County early in January, for Texas. There were in all six families, viz.: JAMES G. POWELL, wife and eight children; LEWIS COWART, wife and seven children; JEPTHA V. WALKER, wife and five children; MRS. JONES and her two sons and two daughters; MRS. HILL, HENRY HILL and MISS REBECCA HILL. The party proceeded in safety until they reached N. Orleans, where they embarked aboard a steamer...Mr. Cowart was taken sick with the cholera and died in a few hours. His comrades and family landed to perform the last rites of burial, when the entire company were prostrated with the disease in its most malignant form. Mr. Cowart, his youngest child, and a nephew by the name of WRIGHT, were among the earliest victims. Mr. James G. Powell is also among the dead. At the latest advances, eighteen of the company had been buried - seven negroes in one grave!...

Died at Milledgeville on the evening of the 4th inst., FORT, second son of John HAMMOND, Esq., aged three years.

Proclamation by Gov. George W. Towns offering $150 reward for the apprehension of Benjamin S. Brantly for murder committed upon the body of JAMES MORRIS in Washington county on the 2d of December last...

17 Apr 1849

Departed this life in Talbot county on Thursday evening the fifth inst., in the 35th year of her age, MRS. LOUISA BARKSDALE, daughter of Samuel and Lucy Barksdale of Warren county, and wife of John E. Barksdale, Esq. (eulogy)

1 May 1849

Departed this life on the 17th inst. at her residence in the county of Putnam, MRS. ELIZABETH INGRAM, consort of Mr. Presly Ingram, in the 68th year of her age. (long eulogy)

THOMAS A. COOPER, Esq., the celebrated tragedian, the scholar and the gentleman, died on Sat. last at the house of his son-in-law, Mr. Robert Tyler, in Bristol, Pennsylvania. (Wash. Union, 25th ult)

8 May 1849

We regret to see in the Charleston papers an announcement of the death of HENRY BAILEY, Esq., a distinguished member of the Charleston Bar, and for many years Attorney General of South Carolina.

22 May 1849
   Proclamation by Gov. George W. Towns offering $150 reward for the
   apprehension of Robert McCarthy for murder committed upon the body of
   ANDREW BAKER. McCarthy has escaped from the Jail of Baker County...

29 May 1849
   Died in this city on the 17th inst., VICTORIA COTTON, aged 10 years
   11 months.

   From the New Orleans Picayune. Details of the death of Major Gen.
   W. J. WORTH, who died in San Antonio on Tuesday last, the 8th inst. at
   half past 1 o'clock P.M. (it should be Monday, the 7th)...

   From the Journal & Messenger. Committed for trial. Elisha Reese, charged
   with the murder of MRS. PRATT, in this county on Wed. last, was arrested
   the same evening...

   DAN MARBLE, the well known personator of Yankee character, died of cholera
   at Louisville on the 15th ult. So says a telegraphic despatch received at
   Boston on Tuesday, by W. Warren, Esq., of the Boston Museum.

   The HON. DANIEL DUNCAN, of Ohio, died in Washington on Friday evening at
   half past five o'clock.

   Murder. We regret to learn that COL. DAVID ROSS, of Putnam county, was
   shot and instantly killed about 9 o'clock on Monday night last while
   passing from his mill on the Oconee to his residence, a distance of about
   half a mile. The assassin was unknown.

5 June 1849
   Died near his residence in Putnam county on Monday night the 21st ult.,
   COL. DAVID ROSS, aged 52 years. Col. Ross fell by the hands of some
   unknown assassin...was a native of Hancock co. but a resident of Putnam
   county for many years previous to his death; in 1836 he commanded a
   battalion of horse against the Seminole Indians. (eulogy) (The Southern
   Recorder and Macon Telegraph will please copy)

   Died at his residence in this county on the 18th ult., MR. SOLOMON BANKS,
   about 72 years of age; member of the Baptist Church (short eulogy).

   Departed this life at his residence in Jones County on Thursday morning
   the 24th ult. in the 67th year of his age, MR. HENRY FINNEY. Had been the
   subject of affliction for the last four years of Palsy.

   Died in Monticello on Tuesday 22d ult. of a protracted illness, MR. SAMUEL A.
   FLOURNOY, aged 49 years. Was a native of Chesterfield county, Va., but for
   several years past a resident of this village. (The Richmond papers will
   please copy)

   The New Orleans papers announce the death of MR. GEORGE PORTER, Associate
   Editor of the Picayune, after a brief illness.

12 June 1849
     Died on the fourth of April last at his residence in Greene county,
     MOSES JACKSON, in the 83d year of his age.

     A telegraph despatch to the Charleston Courier from New Orleans says
     that Maj. Gen. EDMUND PENDLETON GAINES breathed his last at the St. Charles
     Hotel, New Orleans, at 3 o'clock on Wed. morning, of Cholera, after an
     illness of only a day or two.

     The St. Louis Union says that MR. FRANKLIN A. POGUE, a young man of much
     promise, was recently killed at Louisiana, Mo. ...

19 June 1849
     From Texas. The Bonham Advertiser states that a MRS. CHESHIRE and
     MR. CRAWFORD, both residing about five miles above Dallas, were killed
     by lightning on the night of the 4th ult.

     From Texas. Captain EDWARD DEAS, 4th Artillery, stationed at Camp Ringgold,
     was drowned from on board the steamer Yazoo, near Rio Grande City, on the
     26th ultimo. Captain Deas had served on both lines during the Mexican war,
     and was taken prisoner shortly sfter the battles of the 8th and 9th of May.
     His brother, Deas, was Assistant Adjutant-General to the late General Worth,
     commandant of the 8th Military Dept.

     Col. HENRY W. JERNIGAN died at his residence in Alabama on the 2d inst.,
     in the 43d year of his age; for several years a member of the State
     Legislature (eulogy) (Columbus Enquirer)

     Murder of Col. DAVID ROSS. Some days ago we gave an account of the
     assassination of Col. David Ross, of Putnam, in going from his mill to his
     house. At the inquest held over his body, his own son, a youth of 20 years of
     age, was found guilty of the murder. A negro girl belonging to the deceased
     has been lodged in jail, charged as accessory to his murder. (Augusta
     Republic, 12th inst.)

     Died at her residence in this county on the morning of the 13th inst.,
     MRS. MARY WHITAKER, consort of Wm. Whitaker, deceased, in the 60th year of
     her age; member of the Baptist Church (eulogy)

     Died at his residence in Forsyth county on the 30th of May last, GEORGE
     WOODLIFF, Esq., aged 63 years, after a short but most virulent attack of
     Bronchitis. Was a native of Henry county, Virginia, whence he removed to
     this State about 35 years ago; for six years previous to his death he was
     an acceptable member of the Methodist Episcopal Church.

     Proclamation by Gov. George W. Towns offering $150 reward for the apprehension
     of Isham Cooper for murder committed upon the body of WILLIAM HAGWOOD in Dade
     County on the 2d inst. ...

26 June 1849
     Died at his Plantation in this county on Thursday last, Major RICHARD ROWELL,
     in the 68th year of his age. He was born in Greenville Co., Virginia and
     removed to this State in 1805. (eulogy)

Outrageous murder. On the night of the 8th inst., SIMEON FULLER, of
Greene county, brutally murdered, supposed, by two men of the name of
William Hamilton Hall and John Hall, of Louisiana, brothers. It appears
that the deceased married their mother, by whom he obtained some negroes
and other property. After the decease of the mother, the sons came to this
State and demanded the property...have since been arrested at Covington,
in Newton county, about 15 miles from the scene of the murder. (Jeffersonian)

Death of ex-President JAMES K. POLK.

3 July 1849
    Died on the 26th June at Blountsville, Jones county (the place of his
    family residence), Major FRANCIS TUFTS, in the 70th year of his age. Was
    born and raised in Massachusetts, moved to Savannah, Geo. when a young man,
    and moved from there to this county some 25 years ago; left a wife and seven
    children.

    Departed this life in Macon county, Alabama on the 9th June, aged 24 years
    7 months 12 days, MRS. MARY, consort of Dr. Wm. G. SWANSON and daughter of
    Gen. John W. Burney of Monticello, Geo.; leaves husband and babe (eulogy).

    A Fatal duel took place yesterdat at ten o'clock, six miles above this
    city on the Indiana shore, between two well known citizens of Louisville,
    Mr. John T. Grey and Capt. HENRY C. POPE...resulting in the death of the
    latter (Louisville Journal, June 15)

10 Jul 1849
    Captain JAMES MISSROON, one of our oldest and most respected citizens,
    died on Sullivan's Island on Wed. evening, in the 78th year of his age. He
    was for many years in command of vessels engaged in the Charleston trade.
    (Chas. Mer. 29th June)

    Died in Newton county on the 17th of June, MRS. OLIVE LEE, wife of
    Nathan P. Lee, in the 46th year of her age. She was taken with paralysis
    and lived about three days afterward; member of the Baptist Church; leaves
    husband and children (long eulogy)

17 Jul 1849
    Died on 16th June in Glennville, Alabama, MARY ELIZABETH, aged 9 months and
    a few days, daughter of Joseph S. and Antoinett C. POWELL.

    From the Savannah Republican. Remarkable instance of longevity...her name was
    MRS. LOURANIA THROWER. She died on the 29th of March 1849 at her residence in
    Scriven county, on the Ogechee, near the Rail Road, between the sixty and
    seventy mile stations, where she had lived for many years. Her age is
    considered by her relations to be 133 years, and from all accounts given by
    herself she must have been that at least...was born in Virginia, moved from
    that State to North Carolina, and from North Carolina she moved to this State
    and settled in Scriven county, which was Effingham county at that time. Had
    seven children - six daughters and one son - all of whom were born before the
    Revolution; survived by three daughters - two live in this county and one in
    Florida. The youngest of her children is between 70-80 years old; has
    grandchildren that are getting quite aged; has great great grandchildren that
    are 30 years old; has great great great grandchildren the ages of whom we
    have not been able to ascertain, as they reside in Florida; member of the
    Baptist Church.

A venerable and amiable pair. It is with deep regret (says the Washington Union) that John Y. Mason, Esq., the late Secretary of the Navy, has lost in less than one month both his excellent parents. They lived and died in Greensville County, Virginia, on the same farm and at the same house where they had settled in 1792, soon after their marriage. MR. EDMUNDS MASON died on the 27th May last, in the 80th year of his age; and his wife on the 22d June, in the 76th year of her age. They had been married 50 years.

The Mobile Herald and Tribune of the 4th inst. says - After an illness of some ten days, COL. DUNCAN, Inspector General of the US Army, died at the Mansion House in this city at 2 o'clock yesterday morning. His disease, we learn, was fever, contracted by exposure to the intense heat in a journey on horseback from Mount Vernon Arsenal to this city.

A despatch from our Baltimore correspondent, under date of 12th instant, brings us the melancholy intelligence of the death of MRS. MADISON, wife of ex-President Madison. She died in Washington city on the morning of the tenth.

24 Jul 1849

Died at Irwinton, Ga. on the 15th inst., ANN ELIZA, infant daughter and only child of James C. and Martha E. BOWER, three days less than three months old.

31 Jul 1849

Died in Jasper county on the 20th July, MRS. MARY RAMEY, wife of William Ramey, Esq., in the 48th year of her age; member of the Baptist Church.

Died in Columbus, Ga. on the 11th inst., MRS. ELOISE, wife of Thomas B. GOULDING, and daughter of the Hon. John A. and Mrs. Louisa Cuthbert, of Mobile, Ala.

21 Aug 1849

Tribute of Respect by Sylvan Lodge No. 4 I.O.O.F., Milledgeville, dated August 10, 1849 - on the death of GEORGE W. FENN.

28 Aug 1849

Departed this life on the 18th inst. in the town of Clinton, JAMES M. GRAY, Esq., in the 61st year of his age; for many years a representative of this County in the State Legislature, and long a member of the Inferior Court. (eulogy)

SIMON WHITAKER is no more! In the 69th year of his age, on the morning of the 7th inst., at his residence in Fayette Co....he breathed his last; a member of the Baptist Church; his remains have been laid beside those of the wife of his youth.

Died at Midway near this city on Sat. inst. in the 61st year of his age, RICHARD J. NICHOLS, Esq., one of the oldest, most respected and esteemed members of this community.

Died in Dahlonega on the 10th inst., COL. STEPHEN D. CRANE, aged 48 years.

Died in Lumpkin on the 3d inst., BENJ. W. CLARKE, aged 24 years.

4 Sep 1849
  Departed this life on the 26th ult. after a long and painful illness,
  STERLING W. SMITH, SR., Esqr., in the 67th year of his age - a native
  of Brunswick county, Va. but for the last 30 years a resident of Jones
  county...Judge Smith was a highminded and intelligent farmer and devoted
  his life mainly to agricultural pursuits.

  Departed this life on the 11th ult. in the 26th year of her age,
  MRS. CATHARINE L. DOGGET, wife of Jessie Dogget and daughter of Sterling W.
  Smith, Sr., Esq., since deceased. She has left two small children, a
  husband and numerous relatives to mourn their untimely loss.

11 Sep 1849
  Died on Wed. August 29th at Stone Mountain, MRS. SARAH S. JENKINS,wife
  of Charles J. Jenkins, Esq., of Augusta, in the 44th year of her age. But
  a few brief months have passed away since the hand of affection recorded
  the untimely decease of her two beloved children... (eulogy)

  Died of a paralytic affection on the morning of the 29th ult., MR. SAMUEL
  BUFFINGTON, SENR., one of the earliest and oldest citizens of Milledgeville.

  Fatal rencontre. We understand that on Saturday the 1st inst. at Jacksonville,
  in Telfair county, a rencontre took place between Dr. Humphreys and
  Dr. T.F. MOORE. Our informant states that after each had snapped a pistol
  at the other, Dr. Moore retired, when Dr. H. seized a double barreled gun,
  fired one barrel without effect, and immediately fired the other, which
  lodged ten buck shot in the back of Dr. Moore, who died the following day...
  Dr. Moore was a printer, learned his trade in this office, and until the
  last eight months was for several years its foreman...leaves aged mother.

  ELISHA REECE, who at the July Term of Bibb Superior Court, was convicted of
  the murder of MRS. PRATT on Friday last at Macon, suffered the penalty of
  the law. The Museum says the execution took place "in the presence of several
  thousand persons, of all grades and both sexes."

  We are pained to learn that the Hon. EDWARD J. BLACK, of Scriven, is no
  more! He has for several terms been a member of the Legislature, and for
  several years an able and influential member of Congress. He died on the
  1st inst. at Barnwell, South Carolina.

  The last mail brought us the painful intelligence that Gen. DANIEL McDOUGALD
  of Columbus died at that city on Saturday last. His disease was typhus fever.

18 Sep 1849
  Died in Twiggs county on Wed. the 5th day of September at 7 o'clock P.M.,
  in the 16th year of her age, MISS MARY ANN BURNS, eldest child of Mr. and Mrs.
  James C. Burns; member of the Baptist Church (eulogy).

  Truly the afflicting hand of Providence has fallen heavily upon Mr. and Mrs.
  BURNS. On the morning of the 6th inst., just ten hours after the death of
  MARY, died CORNELIA, their infant child - aged 6 months. (eulogy)

  Died in this county on the 21st ult. in the 41st year of his age, of Typhoid
  fever, JOHN O. PROSSER, leaving a wife and eight children.

25 Sep 1849
   Tribute of Respect by Sylvan Lodge No. 4 I.O.O.F., Milledgeville, dated
   Sep. 18, 1849 - on the death of TOMLINSON F. MOORE.

2 Oct 1849
   Departed this life at his residence in Monroe county on the 13th inst.,
   SIMON HOLT, in the 69th year of his age.

   It is our painful duty to announce the death of P.C. GIEU, Esq., the
   former able and efficient Editor of the Constitutionalist; he died in
   Augusta on Sat. morning last. Was a native of St. Domingo and came to
   this country when a young man.

9 Oct 1849
   Sad accident. The Muscogee Democrat of the 4th inst. says - On Monday
   last one of the Stage Drivers, on the route from this place to Barnesville,
   was instantly crushed to death by the upsetting of the stage he was
   driving, he being thrown under the falling vehicle at the moment of the
   accident. The name of the unfortunate man was COOPER, and was recently
   from Ohio- One of the lady passengers, Mrs. Mitchell, of Montgomery county,
   Ala., was considerably injured by the upsetting of the Stage, not, we hope,
   dangerously.

23 Oct 1849
   Tribute of Respect by Irwinton Division No. 96 Sons of Temperance, dated
   Sep. 29th, 1849 - on deaths of JOEL H. ETHERIDGE and WESLEY A. FISHER.

   Proclamation by Gov. George W. Towns offering $150 reward for the apprehension
   of Marcus B. Fambrough for murder committed upon the body of HIRAM L. STORY
   in Coweta county on Tuesday night the 2d instant...

30 Oct 1849
   MR. JOHN G. PONDER, from Richmond, Virginia, on his way to Florida, with a
   number of negroes, was murdered about ten miles below Hawkinsville, Ga. on
   Sunday night 21st inst., but no suspicion rests upon the negroes, as being
   implicated in the act.

   A tragical event. The Augusta Chronicle of Thursday says that Bennett Dozier,
   an inmate of the Hospital in this city, said to be laboring under delirium
   tremens, stabbed and killed MR. THOMAS HARDAWAY, and severely wounded the
   keeper of the Hospital, Mr. Charles T. Rich...Mr. Hardaway was 23 years of
   age, and leaves a wife to mourn his sudden and tragical death.

13 Nov 1849
   Died on Tuesday night the 6th inst. at Lawrenceville, Georgia, of Consumption,
   HINES HOLT, eldest son of Col. Nathan L. and Mrs. Mary D. HUTCHINS, aged
   20 years.

20 Nov 1849
   Fatal accident. Letter headed Troupville, Lowndes Co., Nov. 10, 1849. -
   giving details of the death of SEABORN JONES (Allen Jones' brother) due to
   the accidental discharge of a gun in the hands of his son William Jones.

Died in this city on Wed. last Nov. 14th, MR. JAMES O'BRIEN, in the 56th year of his age. Was a native of Dublin, Ireland where he was born 2d July 1793. He left his native land for this country at the age of 23 - has been a citizen of this place upwards of 30 years. For some time previous to his death, it was his misfortune to lose God's highest gift to man, (reason)...

Proclamation by Gov. George W. Towns offering $100 reward for the apprehension of Thomas Burge for murder committed upon the body of RICHARD ALTMAN in the city of Macon on the 15th day of November instant...

27 Nov 1849
Died at the residence of his brother Thos. P. Hughs, in the county of Wilkinson, IVERSON G. HUGHES, youngest son of the late Rev. John Hughs and Margaret Hughs, now Mrs. Tharpe, on the 19th year of his age. (short eulogy)

30 Nov 1849 - Extra
Death of Gen. CLINCH. This gentleman died at Macon on Tuesday last.

4 Dec 1849
Departed this life on the 27th ult. in the 66th year of her age, CATHARINE GUMM, wife of Jacob Gumm, Senr.; for the last 20 years a member of the M.E. Church; for last 30 years under the care of physician Dr. Fort. (eulogy) (North Carolina papers please copy)

Died in Madison Co., Ga. on Tuesday the 20th of Nov 1849, MRS. ELIZABETH DANIEL, wife of Capt. James Daniel, aged 39 years; leaves husband and children.

Died in this county on the 24th ult., MRS. CATHERINE S. BONNER, in the 61st year of her age; for last 45 years a member of the Methodist Episcopal Church (eulogy).

11 Dec 1849
Died in Griffin on the 5th inst. of Inflammatory Rheumatism, after a protracted illness, MR. F. GREEN; leaves a wife and two children.

The last Columbus Enquirer came to us shrouded in mourning on account of the decease of GEORGE W. HARDWICK, long one of its proprietors and Editors. Was a graduate of the University in this vicinity.

18 Dec 1849
Died in Milledgeville on the morning of the 6th inst., MRS. MARTHA DOLES, wife of Mr. Josiah Doles - leaving husband, two sons, and four small daughters, three brothers and four sisters. (long eulogy)

One of the band of enterprising young men who left this city last Spring for California is no more. MR. ELLSWORTH F. PARK died on the 9th of September at the big bar, on the Middle Fork of the American River, thirty miles above Sutter's Mills. A graduate of Oglethorpe University, he had been admitted to the bar but...became an adventurer for fame and fortune in California.

25 Dec 1849

Departed this life on the 22d Nov. in the 70th year of his age, CAPT. EDWARD J. TARPLEY, formerly of Brunswick county, Va. Was born in Brunswick county and partly raised in Charlotte Co, Va, In 1800 he intermarried with Mary B. Manson of Brunswick county; raised a large family of children and in 1834 emigrated to Wilkinson County, Ga., where he resided till his death. In the month of June he was taken sick with the ordinary fever of the country...leaves wife and children (long eulogy).

Died at Macon on Tuesday last, MRS. ELIZA RANDOLPH, relict of the late Dr. R. H. Randolph.

Died suddenly at his residence in Houston county, on Thursday last, MR. DANIEL GUNN.

Died suddenly in this city yesterday morning, COL. RICHARD BLOUNT, one of the oldest and most esteemed members of this community.

1 Jan 1850

Died at his residence in this city on the 24th of December, COL. RICHARD BLOUNT, in the 76th (?) year of his age. Was born in Southampton, Virginia and emigrated to Georgia in 1802. He represented Hancock county in the first Legislature held in this city; professed Methodist religion for more than forty years (eulogy).

8 Jan 1850

Information wanted. Died at my residence in this Village on the 13th of December last, an aged lady by the name of ELIZABETH SAWYER, leaving some personal property which her legal representative can have by making application. She stated that she had relatives living in Milledgeville, Georgia, and in Florida. Signed Wm. J. Knauff, Pendleton Co., SC Jan 3, 1850. (The Federal Union and Floridian (Tallahassee, Florida) will copy once)

15 Jan 1850

It is with profound sorrow we announce the death of CHARLES H. RICE, Esq., one of the Secretaries of the Executive Department. He died at his residence in this city on Sunday evening last, of Typhoid fever, after an illness of about ten days. (short eulogy)

Died at the residence of his father in Bibb county on the 12th inst., MR. JAS. S. BIVINS, son of Roland Bivins, Esq....but months since the deceased became a graduate of Oglethorpe University (short eulogy).

Departed this life in this city on the 12th instant, MRS. MARIA COTTON, wife of Thomas Cotton, in the 45th year of her age. Was a native of England but had been a resident of this city about 8 years.

22 Jan 1850

Departed this life on the 9th inst. in Jasper county, LEWIS PHILLIPS, Esq., in the 68th year of his age. Was a native of North Carolina and emigrated to said county about 38 years ago. His death was occasioned by a cancer.

Departed this life on the 24th ult. at his residence in Lowndes county, Ga., of pneumonia, Maj. FRANCIS JONES, in the 58th year of his age; for nearly 20 years a citizen of this county (eulogy).

Index to Deaths from the Federal Union (Milledgeville, GA.)

Index to Deaths from the Federal Union (Milledgeville, GA.)

Index to Deaths from the Federal Union (Milledgeville, GA.)

Index to Deaths from the Federal Union (Milledgeville, GA.)

Index to Deaths from the Federal Union (Milledgeville, GA.)

Index to Deaths from the Federal Union (Milledgeville, GA.)

Index to Deaths from the Federal Union (Milledgeville, GA.)

Index to Deaths from the Federal Union (Milledgeville, GA.)

Index to Deaths from the Federal Union (Milledgeville, GA.)

Index to Deaths from the Federal Union (Milledgeville, GA.)

Index to Deaths from the Federal Union (Milledgeville, GA.)

Index to Deaths from the Federal Union (Milledgeville, GA.)

Index to Deaths from the Federal Union (Milledgeville, GA.)

Index to Deaths from the Federal Union (Milledgeville, GA.)

Index to Deaths from the Federal Union (Milledgeville, GA.)

Index to Deaths from the Federal Union (Milledgeville, GA.)

Index to Deaths from the Federal Union (Milledgeville, GA.)

Index to Deaths from the Federal Union (Milledgeville, GA.)

www.ingramcontent.com/pod-product-compliance
Lightning Source LLC
Chambersburg PA
CBHW032043040426
42334CB00038B/571